PLAIN
TALK
ON
Thessalonians

PLAIN
TALK
ON
Thessalonians

MANFORD GEORGE GUTZKE
PH.D.

ZONDERVAN
PUBLISHING HOUSE OF THE ZONDERVAN CORPORATION
GRAND RAPIDS, MICHIGAN 49506

PLAIN TALK ON THESSALONIANS
Copyright © 1980 by The Zondervan Corporation

Library of Congress Cataloging in Publication Data

Gutzke, Manford George.
  Plain talk on Thessalonians.

   1. Bible.   N.T.   Thessalonians—Commentaries.
I. Title.
BS2725.3.G87   227'.8107   80-10119
ISBN 0-310-25701-8

Printed in the United States of America

Contents

FIRST THESSALONIANS

FIRST THESSALONIANS
Chapter 1

† † †

SALUTATION
(1 Thess. 1:1)

Can you understand why at times Paul wrote only to believers?

> Paul, and Silvanus, and Timotheus, unto the church of the Thessalonians which is in God the Father and in the Lord Jesus Christ: Grace be unto you, and peace, from God our Father, and the Lord Jesus Christ (1 Thess. 1:1).

If I installed an outboard motor on a boat that I ordinarily used with oars, can you see that I would be in a different situation? If I took the elevator to get to the sixth floor of a building instead of walking up the stairs, I would also be in a different situation. Even so, if one has accepted Christ as Savior and has Christ in him, life is all different.

By "the church of the Thessalonians" Paul means the group of believers in Christ Jesus who lived in the city and region of Thessalonica. Each of these believers had been born again and had become a new creature in Christ Jesus; old things had passed away and all things had become new. Each had in himself the old man and the new man, the natural man and the spiritual man; and in each case the new man, the spiritual man, needed to be fed.

The natural man is fed by the food that he eats, but the new man needs to be fed by the Word of God. This is what Paul undertakes to explain in this epistle.

It appears that the Corinthian church was in many respects the youngest of all spiritually. They were babes in Christ: Paul would say that they were yet carnal. When he uses the word "yet" he implies that they were not to stay that way. When a person first believes in the Lord Jesus Christ, God regenerates—starts a new life inside—and that person becomes a babe in Christ. As long as that person is a babe in Christ, the old or natural man is in control. Paul would say that that person is carnal. He must grow spiritually until the spiritual overcomes the carnal.

In the Book of Galatians, Paul points out that the believer has in him the flesh and the spirit. These two are contrary to one another: they lust against each other.

Compared to the other churches in the epistles of Paul, the one in Thessalonica could be called the normal or typical church. This church was not particularly carnal; the believers there were not particularly deficient in anything. As we read this letter we will learn that they had no apparent problems among themselves, whereas the Corinthian letter deals with one problem after another. The Thessalonian letter has a message that Paul would send to any church or any believer.

Now let us consider what Paul has in mind when he speaks of the church. He is speaking of a group of believers among whom there is a fellowship, a communion, because Christ is in each one. These believers make up the body of Christ, of which He is the head. Christ is therefore directing and guiding them. So Paul addresses them as "the church of the Thessalonians which is in God the Father and in the Lord Jesus Christ." Further, this group is composed of individual believers involved in a relationship that is between God the Father and the Lord Jesus Christ. I think that is seen in the words, "in God the Father and in the Lord Jesus Christ."

When we speak of God the Father, we are not speaking of God the Creator of the universe. (He is that, but not especially in this connection.) He is the Father in the sense that He is the one who begot the believers. They are born again and He is their Father.

This church is also in the Lord Jesus Christ; every believer is a member of the body of Christ, and He is the head of each one. Any believer can take this epistle to himself in an awareness of belonging to the church, because every believer in the Lord Jesus Christ is a member of that body. He is a fellow laborer with all other believers; he is not alone. It is wonderful to know that he does not have to be alone. But it is also wonderful to see that he is responsible to other believers.

"Paul, and Silvanus, and Timotheus" are sending this letter to the believers who are in Thessalonica, who constitute the church there—not because they meet in one place, but because they belong together in the Father and in the Lord Jesus Christ.

"Grace be unto you, and peace, from God our Father, and the Lord Jesus Christ." When Paul writes "grace be unto you," he is not referring to that grace by which they are saved (because God in His mercy will receive believers even when they are not worthy); he refers instead to that grace that God gives to believers after they are saved. Paul referred to this in writing to the believers at Rome when he said that they had "access by faith into this grace wherein we stand." What did he mean?

When a person is a believer in the Lord Jesus Christ and is following His guidance, the Lord will lead him into what he should do: namely, how to deny and yield himself, and how to accept what is happening; how to be meek, how to be humble, and how to depend upon God. Humanly speaking, the believer could not do that even if he tried. He would in some way be selfish; he would be concerned with his own wishes and needs. So grace—the divine enablement by which the believer responds in obedience to the will of God in order to serve Christ—is given to him.

"And peace"—that is a wonderful word that almost everybody understands. All is at rest: no inner turmoil, no outer fear, enemies are overcome by the living Lord.

"From God our Father," who no longer holds anything against the believer. "And the Lord Jesus Christ," who bears the believer's burdens. This first verse in the first epistle to the Thessalonians makes us aware that salvation is a gift. We thank the Lord for it.

THE TRAITS OF A BELIEVER
(1 Thess. 1:2-4)

Do you know why a believer should thank God for other believers?

> We give thanks to God always for you all, making mention of
> you in our prayers; remembering without ceasing your work of
> faith, and labor of love, and patience of hope in our Lord Jesus
> Christ, in the sight of God and our Father; knowing, brethren
> beloved, your election of God (1 Thess. 1:2-4).

Paul always gave thanks to God for the believers because he knew that God had saved them. When he remembered how they lived their lives, he realized God was working in them to will and to do of His good pleasure. The very fact that there were other people who believed enabled him to understand that it is God who produces these results.

We might keep this in mind when we talk to other people, seeking to win them. Often we end up feeling that it is up to us to convince them; so we bring forth all the arguments we can to prove that the Bible is true and the gospel, real, and that the power of God is great. We need to remember that it is God who convinces. We need only to declare the gospel, to witness to the work of Jesus Christ; God gives the faith and persuades the person to trust in Him.

Paul made mention of these believers individually in prayer. We often pray for someone who is in difficulty: we ought also to thank God for those who are obedient and are serving Him. Ordinarily, when we think of praying for others, we think mainly of those who are badly in need. But from what we see here, this is inadequate. We should be thanking God for all people who believe, making mention of them and calling them to mind.

We may wonder if Paul had a prayer list. I am not sure; he did not mention one. This may not have been necessary for him, although it is not a bad idea.

A prayer list can be a fine reminder of what you want to do. You will want to thank God for those who believe, remembering "without ceasing" that He has done things in others, for others, and through others. You should remember those who are sick, and those who are erring and straying. But you should also pray for the people who have done God's will, who are faithful to Him.

Do you know what "without ceasing" means? It means that we are to thank God again and again, and, yes—again. God knows, but I need to recall what He has done for that man who is now a strong witness for Him. I need to remember what He has done for that woman who has been kept out of trouble, whose testimony is straight and clear and strong, because of her faith in the Lord Jesus Christ. I should remember such people and thank God for them.

Now Paul points to three characteristics of the Thessalonian believers. He writes of remembering their "work of faith." That sounds so ordinary. But we can run into real difficulty trying to understand this matter of faith. There are many persons who think that if they say they believe, that is all that is required of them. If they say they believe, we are supposed to mark it down that they believe. But do they believe? James writes that "faith without works is dead."

I am glad that Paul emphasizes in his epistles that salvation is not a matter of faith and works (that is, my works). It is not a matter of having faith in God and then doing everything I possibly can. That is not the way of blessing. Saving faith is a faith in God that works. If my faith does not lead me to work, it is not real. Toward the end of his second chapter, James spells this out very plainly.

My faith is to be exercised in my living and in my actions. I must do certain things because I believe, and I must expect certain things because I believe.

"And labor of love." This emphasizes an important truth: love is action, not sentiment. Many people think that love is a very sweet, kindly feeling—in fact, not only a kindly feeling but a glowing feeling. That is all very fine in its place, but feelings can pass very quickly. In his first epistle John writes, "Let us not love in word, neither in tongue; but in deed and in truth" (1 John 3:18). Paul emphasizes this aspect when he uses the word "labor"—your "labor of love."

Paul also refers to "patience of hope." Hope is confident expectation that certain consequences will follow. "Patience of hope" is the patience that we show as we wait for the results that we feel sure will come. It is a certain kind of stick-to-itiveness. We really expect results, and we keep on waiting and looking and praying and serving because we do expect them. That word "patience" is not the same as the word "long-suffering"; it means continuing through to the end.

Again, these are three characteristics that we should find in a believer: a "work of faith"—actually something that he does because he believes in God; a "labor of love"—continuing all the way through, doing for others, doing toward God; and "patience of hope."

Paul sums it all up with these words: "knowing, brethren beloved, your election of God." The word is "election," not "selection." Anybody who has been called by God and who responds to that call is "elect." Those who respond in faith are the "called out" ones; they are the "elect" ones. Paul knew that these believing people in Thessalonica really had been called out by God because of their testimony.

THE PATTERN FOR EVANGELISM
(1 Thess. 1:5)

Have you ever considered how Paul thought the gospel should be communicated to unbelievers?

> For our gospel came not unto you in word only, but also in power, and in the Holy Ghost, and in much assurance; as ye know what manner of men we were among you for your sake (1 Thess. 1:5).

Evangelism is the activity whereby the gospel of the Lord Jesus Christ is proclaimed to people who do not know it. In the above verse Paul lists several aspects of a typical case of evangelism. Each may not appear in every case today to the extent that it did with the apostle Paul, but all will be involved.

"For our gospel came not unto you in word only." Many feel that after they have gone to church and listened to preaching they can just live on for another week until it is church time again. But when one goes to church and hears the

Word of God preached, he is told to do something. He is to accept what he has heard as a course of action for himself, and then go out and live it in the days that follow.

To be saved by faith means to be saved by believing the promises of God, but something more is required. One must believe God's promises into action. Believing the gospel as if it were a sign on a wall is not enough. Assenting to the words that I have heard, saying, "Yes, that is true," is not enough. But taking those words as guidance for my actions, and responding to them: that is what true faith is.

> For whosoever shall call upon the name of the Lord shall be saved. How then shall they call on him in whom they have not believed? and how shall they believe in him of whom they have not heard? and how shall they hear without a preacher (Rom. 10:13-14)?

The promises of God that are set forth in so many words need to be preached forthrightly so that they can be believed; that is, so that the hearer can respond to them, and the soul be saved. This is not difficult to do, and it is practical. Here Paul emphasizes "not in word only, but also in power." The Word of God is to be preached in power.

It is difficult to visualize what power means because power cannot be seen. It is not something that can be pressed out of a tube. Power is a measure of the strength or effectiveness of something. When we say "preached in power" we mean preached effectively, impressively. Neither a stiff, formal speech nor a casual, offhand talk has much power. Nor does an impersonal lecture have a great deal of power. To be powerful, effective, preaching must be personally applied.

"And in the Holy Ghost." Have you ever wondered what it means to preach in this manner? Some would say that because they are not ministers, this does not concern them. But do they have children in the home? Do they have neighbors? If so, they are preaching. How then should they go about preaching "in the Holy Ghost"? Consider these words to mean "as led by the Holy Spirit." If people are conscious of the presence of God; if they live their lives in awareness of the indwelling Holy Spirit; and if, as they go about their personal affairs, they walk constantly with Christ; that would be preaching in the Holy Spirit.

The work of the Holy Spirit is to take the things of Christ and show them to us. The preacher, then, will not just use his own ideas, but will do what he is doing in the conscious presence of the Lord Jesus Christ.

"And in much assurance." Paul was absolutely sure the gospel was true. Not only was he sure that the Bible is the Word of God; he was sure that God would work with him. When Paul preached the gospel, he did so with the confident expectation that God would work in the hearts of his hearers. He believed that God would do things that even he, the preacher, would not know about.

"As ye know what manner of men we were among you for your sake." In the next section we shall find out more about this. Paul believed that Scripture as written was the Word of God; that the power that would transform lives was the power of God; that the Holy Spirit of God would be present; and that what he was preaching was absolutely true. These convictions were confirmed in his conduct.

The "manner of man" that the evangelist is makes a great deal of difference in his ministry. If a preacher says things casually or apologetically, giving the impression that he is not sure whether they are right or wrong, his preaching will not be effective.

Paul's evangelism, then, was characterized by these things: words, of which no one need be ashamed; power, believing in the effectiveness of God's working; the Holy Spirit, walking with Him; and much assurance that God would work with him. Paul could not always be sure that people would listen, or that everything he said would be accepted. But he could be sure that what he was saying was true. "Ye know what manner of men we were among you for your sake." What a marvelous outline this is.

Right in your home or wherever you are, God can use your daily life, your words, and your heart's attitudes to convey the message to others. May God bless you as you seek to be faithful in His sight.

THE TESTIMONY OF PAUL'S CONVERTS
(1 Thess. 1:6-8)

Do you think it makes much difference how believers act toward God in public?

> And ye became followers of us, and of the Lord, having received the word in much affliction, with joy of the Holy Ghost: so that ye were ensamples to all that believe in Macedonia and Achaia. For from you sounded out the word of the Lord not only in Macedonia and Achaia, but also in every place your faith to God-ward is spread abroad; so that we need not to speak any thing (1 Thess. 1:6-8).

Is it wrong for a person to follow his preacher? Some will say that a certain man is a great preacher, but that his people just worship him; that they are following him and not the Lord. But those who followed Paul were also following the Lord.

It is not always a simple matter to receive the Word. Receiving the Word means that a person hears the gospel preached and accepts it. He hears the promises stated, and he believes them. In Thessalonica this brought much affliction. The same thing may happen to any of us. There are always those who will be unhappy and resentful, who will ridicule you and be sarcastic, if you attempt to live by the Bible. Yet we read that the same Thessalonians who had received the Word in much affliction also received it "with joy of the Holy Ghost." Even though they suffered affliction from people, they had the joy of the Lord.

"So that ye were ensamples to all that believe in Macedonia and Achaia." The Thessalonians' response influenced others because their conduct was widely publicized throughout the whole region.

"For from you sounded out the word of the Lord." In the original Greek language the expression translated "sounded out" implies "clanged out, boomed out." It was as if a giant brass cymbal had been hit with a sledge hammer. That was the way the testimony of these Thessalonians was described.

Everybody was talking about these new converts—not only in Macedonia and Achaia, but far and wide. You might think that people today would not talk about spiritual testimony like that. But if something happened in a church so that people actually came to the Lord, changed their ways, and committed themselves to Him, it would be widely talked about.

Why would people talk about it? Because that is human nature. People will go to see a fire regardless of where it is. If there is fire in the church, people will gather around. When someone turns to God in an obvious way, it attracts attention and inspires comment.

"Your faith to God-ward is spread abroad"; notice that it is "your faith toward God." Having confidence in just anything is not especially significant because it is not unusual; even pagans have a kind of faith. Some people have faith in idols, or in good luck charms, or in various other things. Others have faith in themselves. But if a person has faith toward God and takes His Word to be true, that is something to talk about.

There is no reference here to their morality. That would not have attracted undue attention. When one person chooses a higher degree of morality than another, people give that person credit for it and let it go at that. The matter of virtue is similar. Once in awhile we find persons who are so honest that they stand out from all others. They may be noted and appreciated, although not always admired. But that is not what Paul wrote about here. He did not even mention their charity. (He refers to it elsewhere, but not here.)

What the people in Macedonia and Achaia talked about was the faith of these converts. They believed in the invisible God—believed in Him enough to let it make a difference in their conduct; and this was noted.

Paul writes, "so that we need not to speak any thing." He is emphasizing that if there are converts who actually live as the gospel leads them to live; who pray and read the Bible; who trust in God and give to the poor; then it is not necessary to do much talking. Actions speak louder than words.

So then, if one is interested in making an impression on somebody he should act it out. For a believer in Christ, what would that involve? One would go to church on Sunday, read the Bible, and pray. If one is the kind of person who trusts God and gives to missions, he will not have to make a big speech. Such conduct will speak for itself.

This is how it was with the Thessalonians. Their witness was such that their faith in God was talked about everywhere "so

that we need not to speak any thing." We should ask the Lord
to help us walk in such a fashion that people who see us will
realize that we, too, believe in God.

THE CLASSIC BEHAVIOR OF ANY
BELIEVER IN CHRIST
(1 Thess. 1:9-10)

Do you have any idea how a person would act if he believed
in the gospel?

> For they themselves show of us what manner of entering in we
> had unto you, and how ye turned to God from idols to serve the
> living and true God; and to wait for his Son from heaven, whom
> he raised from the dead, even Jesus, which delivered us from
> the wrath to come (1 Thess. 1:9-10).

In the above verses the apostle Paul describes the Thessalonians' response to his ministry of the gospel. He had just
been saying that their witness and testimony had gone out to
the whole area in which they lived. Everywhere people were
talking about the effect that the preaching of the gospel had
had upon these Thessalonians who believed. Here Paul says
"they themselves" (the public as a whole) "show of us" (they
talked about Paul and his co-workers; they actually reported
and repeated to one another) "what manner of entering in we
had unto you" (the effectiveness of Paul's coming to the Thessalonians).

People will talk about spiritual responses. When others respond to the truth of the gospel, and when that response
makes a difference in their conduct, people will talk about it.

It is interesting to note that these people did not talk about
how Paul or Silvanus had preached; they talked about how the
Thessalonians had responded. These converts had turned
from natural things toward God, looking outside themselves
and up to Him for help. No longer did they trust their own
desires and their own strength; they yielded themselves to
God's will.

Someone might ask how to tell whether people were serving the living and true God. Such people would be reverent, worshiping God. They would respect authority. They would be considerate of others, loving their neighbors as themselves. And they would be charitable to the poor, disposed to rescue the perishing.

"And to wait for his Son from heaven." Do you realize that this should be one of the characteristics of a believer? When these people looked toward the future they were not looking toward the success of their personal ventures; they were not filled with ideas about what they or others were going to do. They were conscious of the revelation, the promise given, that God would do something. And they looked for God to do His will.

As these new converts looked toward God, they had one expectation of Him: that He would send the Lord Jesus Christ back. That would be the most important thing that could happen. They did not share the common expectation that there would be some golden age in the future. They had no hope of any human solution to the world's problems. They were looking for the return of the Son of God, whom God had raised from the dead: "even Jesus, which delivered us from the wrath to come."

Are you aware that the apostle Paul very seldom used the word "Jesus" in his epistles? That is, he seldom used the word alone. He speaks of the Lord Jesus; of Jesus Christ, or Christ Jesus; of Jesus the Lord. The time period in which the epistles of Paul, James, Peter, and John were written was different from the time period when the Gospels of Matthew, Mark, Luke, and John were being lived. What was the difference? The Lord Jesus had ascended into heaven and had been glorified.

When the apostle Paul uses the word "Jesus" alone, as he does here, he is emphasizing the physical body of Jesus of Nazareth. The one whom Paul is awaiting from heaven will be the one who was raised from the dead, Jesus of Nazareth. When he speaks of "even Jesus" (and he does not use that expression more than half a dozen times in all the epistles), he is always giving special emphasis to the physical body—to the person who was here as Jesus of Nazareth, the one who is coming back in the same manner in which they saw Him go.

"Which delivered us from the wrath to come." A day of judgment (the day of wrath) is coming, a time when God will deal with disobedience. God is not mocked. The Book of Hebrews tells us that "It is a fearful thing to fall into the hands of the living God." The notion that one can live as he pleases and get away with it is a fraud, a deception. God is on His throne; He is long-suffering and patient; but He is looking toward the day when the Lord Jesus Christ will be the Judge of the living and the dead.

The emphasis at the close of this first chapter is remarkable. It tells us that we should turn to God and wait for His Son, even Jesus, who has delivered us from the wrath to come.

FIRST THESSALONIANS
Chapter 2

† † †

A PREACHER MAY BE REBUFFED
(1 Thess. 2:1-2)

Do you think that a preacher should stop preaching when he is rebuffed?

> For yourselves, brethren, know our entrance in unto you, that it was not in vain: but even after that we had suffered before, and were shamefully entreated, as ye know, at Philippi, we were bold in our God to speak unto you the gospel of God with much contention (1 Thess. 2:1-2).

Paul described his manner of preaching as definite and positive. He noted the profound impact it had had upon the people who had heard and responded. He recalled that his ministry had not unfolded in an easy way; it had been neither simple nor easy for him to preach as he had. His style had been effective: "our entrance in unto you, that it was not in vain." A quiet, gentle style of preaching may be mildly impressive, and it is comfortable to hear. But a direct approach that is clear and positive in its thrust is more likely to yield results.

All preaching of the gospel implies that people are lost. So there must be an element of warning when someone is preaching. If a bridge were washed out on a highway, what sort of warning would be effective? A gentle suggestion that the traveler had better be careful would not be enough. We would expect someone to wave his arms and shout that danger was ahead. But that kind of preaching, that style, is not without danger to the preacher.

Personally, I have no affection for an alarm clock. In the days when I was a pastor I suddenly came to understand the attitude of some in my congregation when it occurred to me that, for them, I was almost serving as an alarm clock. I was trying to wake them up. People do not appreciate that. Similarly, when people walk along the streets they do not like to be told to stop; they do not want to turn around. But later, when they understand why you stopped them—because the bridge was out—they will thank you.

Paul and Silas were arrested when they went to Philippi. They were stripped naked, beaten, thrown into prison, and put into stocks. That is where they were when they were singing psalms of praise to God at midnight. But the hostility of the Philippians had not intimidated Paul, and when he arrived in Thessalonica he went straight to the synagogue to preach.

However, we should not credit Paul, as a human being, with extraordinary courage. We should note what he has to say: "We were bold in our God." God was with him. To walk into the synagogue and tell the people that Jesus of Nazareth, whom the Jews had caused to be put to death, was actually the Messiah, the Son of God, was to face possible rejection and persecution. But Paul, who operated under a spiritual compulsion, went in anyway. In his earlier writings he wrote, "Woe is me if I preach not the gospel." When he thought about God he could face people; he was strengthened by the Lord Himself to preach.

Paul's message was to the point: it was centered in the work of Christ Jesus. The very reason Paul was preaching was because Christ Jesus had died for all people: He had borne their sins away. Christ Jesus had been raised from the dead and had ascended into heaven. Now it was possible for a human being to be saved. This needed to be told. So the apostle Paul stepped out to preach the gospel, the very fiber of a saving faith.

People are not saved because they desire to be what they ought to be. In God's sight all have sinned and come short of the glory of God. "There is none righteous, no, not one." People need to hear that "in the fullness of time God sent forth His Son, born of a woman, born under the law," to suffer and die so that they might be saved. Paul preached to the whole world that "whosoever will may come," and that "whosoever cometh shall in no wise be cast out." That was the basic content of the message that he gave forth "with much contention."

Paul was willing to argue. Certain kinds of arguments, I am sure, are fruitless. But when it comes to discussing whether or not Christ Jesus came; whether or not He was the Son of God; whether or not the Resurrection was real; and whether or not His body actually ascended into heaven; those truths need to be stated regardless of opposition. Paul was perfectly willing to face the consequences when he made such statements.

All this brings us to a better understanding of Paul's manner of preaching. And it leads us to realize that we should pray for our ministers. The next time you are in a church service and your preacher walks into the pulpit, pray that he may be given grace from God. Pray that he will have the strength to declare what Christ Jesus has done, and what that means to us.

It has pleased God to save those who believe by the foolishness of preaching. The kind of preaching that saves is positive, aggressive, factual, straightforward, and honest, telling the truth about Jesus Christ so that people may be saved.

PAUL'S PURPOSE IN PREACHING
(1 Thess. 2:3-6)

Can you understand that when a person is entrusted with an important task he should want to please whoever assigns it to him?

> For our exhortation was not of deceit, nor of uncleanness, nor in guile: but as we were allowed of God to be put in trust with the gospel, even so we speak; not as pleasing men, but God, which trieth our hearts. For neither at any time used we flattering words, as ye know, nor a cloak of covetousness; God is witness: nor of men sought we glory, neither of you, nor yet of others, when we might have been burdensome, as the apostles of Christ (1 Thess. 2:3-6).

These are the words with which Paul described his attitude while preaching. He was sensitive to the way he went about his work. He told the Thessalonians that in his exhortation (that is what he called his preaching) he was prompting them to do something that was not of deceit. He knew that what he preached was the truth.

Paul approached his preaching with certain things in mind: that souls were lost; that they needed to be born again; that they were in darkness; that they did not know which way to go; that they were in distress and burdened. Even though he knew all these things to be true, he realized that such truths might not be very pleasant to hear. People might not want to be told that there were blots on their records. But Paul's preaching was not grounded in deceit: he told the truth.

"Nor of uncleanness." By these words Paul meant that he had no selfish motive. That would have made his preaching unclean. Paul was not scheming to influence his hearers for his own personal advantage. He did not go through the exercise of preaching because he had something ulterior in mind: he had a message to deliver that clearly concerned the people.

"Nor in guile." Paul was not trying to be smooth in order to make a sale. Evidently he felt that his hearers should act on their own initiative in light of what he told them. He set the truth before them and challenged them to respond. Each person could do as he or she wanted to do; Paul treated them all the same.

What sort of message do you expect to hear from your preacher? Do you want him to tell you how to clear up matters in the community? Do you want him to expound on what is going on around you? Do you want him to tell you what sharp insight he has? Or do you want him to tell you what God has done, what God is doing, and what God will do? The gospel Paul preached was not his interpretation of world affairs, nor even his plan for advancing or improving any particular idea or person. People needed to be born again, and only God could take care of that. Under certain conditions God would save them, and Paul set forth what those conditions were.

Paul understood himself to be "allowed of God." He was

allowed of God to preach; he was entrusted with the gospel. That gospel was handed to him as a parcel is given to a parcel delivery service; the package was complete. Thus, Paul preached with a deep sense of his responsibility to God, being careful not to add to or subtract from the gospel message. He knew that when he stood to speak or wrote to the people in Thessalonica, God heard everything he said, and saw everything he wrote.

"Not as pleasing men." This was a critical aspect of Paul's attitude. Any preacher needs to ask himself to which gallery he is performing. Is he preaching as he does because people like it? Because it is in line with tradition? Or because God wants him to do it? When a preacher speaks it is very common for him to wonder, "What will the people think?" Paul put all that aside and, looking up into the face of God, asked what the Lord wanted him to say.

"Which trieth our hearts." God notes how the preacher feels. He examines, tests, and evaluates the attitudes of his heart.

"Neither at any time used we flattering words." This also is a dangerous temptation for a speaker, especially for one to whom words come easily. But few hearers are impressed by flattery. As a general rule, when a speaker flatters them, the hearers put their response in neutral and let their engines idle.

It is largely a mistaken idea that people want to be pleased by the preacher; if they do want to be pleased, they generally do not admit it. People who listen seriously to preaching, want the truth. They can do with it as they please, but they want the preacher to tell the truth. They often secretly despise the flatterer; it is as if they feel that they have been let down. They are inclined to wonder, "Does he think he can get away with smoothing it over in that fashion?"

The Thessalonians had heard Paul preach. Paul challenged them, "Did I ever give you the impression that I was trying to get on your good side when I was speaking?"

"Nor a cloak of covetousness; God is witness." Paul was not seeking any personal benefit or advantage when he preached. Other people could judge whether or not he used flattering words; but they could not necessarily detect covetousness on his part. Yet God knew, and Paul knew that God knew, that Paul was not being moved in that fashion.

"Nor of men sought we glory, neither of you, nor yet of others." This is also a common pitfall for public speakers and public servants. They try to say things in such a way that people will praise them. As sensitive as Paul was, his conscience was clear. He had not trimmed his message in order to please anyone.

"When we might have been burdensome, as the apostles of Christ." Paul could have looked to the believers for help in carrying his load. He could have asked them to do something to help him, but this he refused to do.

PAUL'S FAITHFULNESS WAS GROUNDED IN HIS LOVE FOR HIS HEARERS
(1 Thess. 2:7–9)

Do you realize that to be an effective witness for Christ one must sincerely love one's hearers?

> But we were gentle among you, even as a nurse cherisheth her children: so being affectionately desirous of you, we were willing to have imparted unto you, not the gospel of God only, but also our own souls, because ye were dear unto us (1 Thess. 2:7–8).

This is a remarkable revelation of a pastor's heart, and gives us an idea of what a good pastor experiences. Dealing with human beings about their own ideas, attitudes, thoughts, and aims is what a preacher must do. In so doing he will strike sensitive spots in the hearts of his hearers. Sometimes his remarks will not be acceptable to them. The evangelist, the one who talks to them about accepting the Lord Jesus Christ, may say, "You are a doomed soul, headed for destruction." He may even say, "You are going to hell." This is a shocking confrontation, and it is one of the reasons why some people do not like evangelistic services.

It is natural to think that if a person is decent, honest, and helpful, he is all right. It may be difficult to accept the idea that such a person may be lost, but the truth is: "You must be born again."

We have seen in previous studies that Paul was positive and bold, showing little concern about negative reaction to his preaching. Now we are to see that to those who turned from their idols to serve the living God, Paul was gentle, "even as a nurse cherisheth her children." Consider the nurse's task: the baby cannot have everything it wants. There are things within a baby's sight that the nurse has to be careful to keep away from it. The nurse turns the baby away from danger, gently.

"Being affectionately desirous of you." Paul's heart was involved with those who believed. He sincerely wanted them to be blessed. And if, he could have given anything that would have increased their happiness, that would have been his desire. So he wrote, "We were willing to have imparted unto you, not the gospel of God only, but also our own souls." He would have given anything for them to understand the Lord Jesus Christ. Paul gladly shared the gospel, telling them that God loved them, had sent His Son to die for them, and would receive them as His children. In addition, Paul would gladly have given himself. He did not withold anything because, "you were dear unto us." They were not his family, nor even his fellow laborers. But they belonged to Christ. And because Christ had died for them and bought them with His own blood, they also belonged to Paul.

> For ye remember, brethren, our labor and travail: for laboring night and day, because we would not be chargeable unto any of you, we preached unto you the gospel of God (1 Thess. 2:9).

Elsewhere in the New Testament we have learned that Paul worked at his trade of tentmaking to support himself rather than asking anyone to help him financially. Here he refers to that: Paul would not ask those people to support him. He came with the express purpose of giving them everything that pertained to eternal life, and he wanted to do it freely.

This is strong guidance as to how effective evangelism should be carried on. The message is free; it should be declared freely, at the cost of the evangelist. You and I should keep this in mind when we think of evangelists and those who work with them, recognizing that anyone who contributes to an evangelistic enterprise is sharing in that service.

In the early days of the church, when Paul went on missionary journeys, there were occasions when he did not have support. But there were also times when believers did support him. In writing to the Philippian church he did not forget how they contributed to his needs. But that was not true in every case, and here in Thessalonica no one was helping him. Aquila and Priscilla were also tentmakers, and he worked at his trade while rooming with them: "laboring night and day . . . we preached unto you the gospel of God." Paul gave himself over to his task so that the hearers might have the wonderful truth of the free grace of God in Christ Jesus.

PAUL'S CONDUCT WAS ABOVE REPROACH
(1 Thess. 2:10–12)

Can you understand why it is so important for the public conduct of a witness for Christ to be above reproach?

> Ye are witnesses, and God also, how holily and justly and unblameably we behaved ourselves among you that believe: as ye know how we exhorted and comforted and charged every one of you, as a father doth his children, that ye would walk worthy of God, who hath called you unto his kingdom and glory (1 Thess. 2:10–12).

The public conduct of a preacher is an open book. These remarks by Paul refer to the most important part of his ministry to the believers in Thessalonica. He had lived a careful and responsible life among them. Now he wants them to understand that that was a deliberate part of his witness to them. What he had preached to them was really true. They could be assured of that in part by noting how completely he put himself into what he was doing.

When Paul says that he had conducted himself "holily," he means that he had put all he had into it. He was what they could see and testify about: his record was clear. "And unblameably." This is an inward comment. He was inwardly unselfish, as God would know, with no pride, no self-seeking.

"We behaved ourselves among you that believe." Paul was in charge of himself; he took himself in hand, treated himself as if he were a third person, and saw to it that he was disciplined. This is the crucial test for any believer in his or her own home. We should ask ourselves the question, "What does my own family think about me?"

"As ye know how we exhorted." Paul wanted his converts to walk in the Lord, and he told them so. The language implies that Paul was urgent in his instructions, knowing that the dead weight of the old man (the carnal self) would be in every believer. He exhorted them the way a cheerleader exhorts a team on the field and encourages the supporters to cheer for them: "Fight, team, fight!" Paul went around one to one, so to speak, urging them on.

"And comforted." He not only urged them on; he comforted them as well. In the course of living, believers are certain to encounter evil or pain over which they have no control. Paul would comfort them about such things. He would remind them of the Lord's love and providence, thus strengthening their faith and devotion.

Paul wrote to the Romans, "All things work together for good to them that love God, to them who are the called according to his purpose." Paul was anxious that not one believer be remiss about what he or she could do.

"And charged every one of you." He did not hesitate to spell out duties to be performed for the Lord's sake.

"As a father doth his children." The children belong to the father, and in a very real way the father feels responsible for how they perform.

"That ye would walk worthy of God." To discover how to walk worthy of God, one should turn to verses 2 and 3 in chapter 4 of Ephesians.

"With all lowliness and meekness, with long-suffering, forbearing one another in love; endeavoring to keep the unity of the Spirit in the bond of peace." Such conduct of a believer would be worthy of God.

"Who hath called you unto his kingdom and glory." Believers are called to enter into a relationship with God known as "the kingdom of God." That relationship will be evident to the world because the conduct of believers shows that God is their Father, that they belong to Him. People look at believers and get an impression about God.

Paul's great purpose, then, was to guide his converts into conduct that would be without spot, unblameable. He urged them to walk that way for the sake of the Lord.

UNREASONABLE OPPOSITION TO THE GOSPEL
(1 Thess. 2:13–16)

Do you think that if a person hears the gospel and accepts Christ as Savior and Lord, he need not fear trouble?

> For this cause also thank we God without ceasing, because, when ye received the word of God which ye heard of us, ye received it not as the word of men, but as it is in truth, the word of God, which effectually worketh also in you that believe (1 Thess. 2:13).

Paul was deeply stirred because these believers had received the gospel as he had preached it: as a message from God Himself for them. We might think that this was partly because of the way that Paul presented it, but Paul takes no credit for himself. He simply praises the Thessalonians for hearing him. It seems to me that the same thing applies to a preacher today. If the preacher is faithful in presenting the Scriptures as written, people can rightly heed the message as coming from God.

A warning seems appropriate here: that to treat Scripture as the work of human beings is to diminish it. There is a danger in any handling of Scripture that takes too much time out to discuss the author's style or personal characteristics. Our chief concern should be with what is written.

If someone tells you that a book of Scripture is bound to be limited because the author was limited, stop! Who is the author? Not the person who wrote it. The author is the Holy Spirit of God.

> For ye, brethren, became followers of the churches of God which in Judea are in Christ Jesus: for ye also have suffered like things of your own countrymen, even as they have of the Jews (1 Thess. 2:14).

In receiving Paul's preaching as the Word of God, the Thessalonian Christians were actually following the example of other believers—those of the churches of God in Judea. When Paul identifies the Thessalonian believers and points out why they are like the Judean believers, he does not focus on the way they listen or the kind of people they are. He focuses on what has happened to them.

The Thessalonians were like the churches in Judea because they had suffered as those churches had. They had been persecuted by their countrymen just as the believers in Judea had been persecuted by the Jews. It has always been the case that when people take Scripture as the Word of God, receiving its promises as true, they find opposition in the world. Are we prepared to accept that as believers who obey the Lord we will actually be persecuted? Paul told Timothy, "Yea, and all that will live godly in Christ Jesus shall suffer persecution" (2 Tim. 3:12). A group of believing people may live in Christian love with one another, but this is not something that the world expects.

The reference to the Jews "who both killed the Lord Jesus, and their own prophets, and have persecuted us; and they please not God, and are contrary to all men" (1 Thess. 2:15) reminds us that some of the bitterest persecution of believers can come from apparently religious people. In fact, persons who lead exemplary Christian lives often suffer more criticism from worldly church members than from unbelieving people.

Paul notes that the persecutors of the churches in Judea were not just offensive to God: they were even at odds with other people.

> Forbidding us to speak to the Gentiles that they might be saved, to fill up their sins always: for the wrath is come upon them to the uttermost (1 Thess. 2:16).

It is one of the strange phenomena of church life that there are those who do not attend evangelistic meetings, but who will do everything they can to prevent an evangelistic service from being held. They have no intention of attending, but they will try to keep such meetings from taking place. There are those who will not witness to anyone, but who are critical of personal workers. They do all they can to oppose those believers who are actively seeking to win others to Christ.

Paul found a similar situation in Thessalonica, and I draw it to your attention so that we all might better understand what we have before us if we desire to walk with the Lord.

EVANGELISTS HAVE PERSONAL LOVE FOR THEIR CONVERTS
(1 Thess. 2:17–20)

Can you understand how converts who have been won are the glory and joy of any minister?

> But we, brethren, being taken from you for a short time in presence, not in heart, endeavored the more abundantly to see your face with great desire (1 Thess. 2:17).

Paul considered face to face communion to be of great value. He remembered the Thessalonian believers clearly and thought of them affectionately; he was glad to hear from Timothy's report that they remembered him and were anxious to see him. But even though the report was gratifying, he longed to see them in person.

The personal presence of other believers is important, as is the knowledge of their activities and their deeds. The latter is always inspiring, but getting together with one another is better and more comforting. Though he had been absent in body, Paul made it a point to reassure them that he was not absent in spirit. Paul tried in every way he could to get to see them.

Believers need to cultivate face–to–face relationships with other believers. That may take extra effort. Paul, however, endeavored the more abundantly" to accomplish it, because fellowship with other believers strengthens.

This brings to mind a very important fact: a believer cannot always do what he wants to do when he wants to do it. He should remember that, in addition to the practical problems of his own strength and his own time, there is a cunning enemy who is determined to hinder him in worshiping God and in his fellowship with others.

Satan is a real being, active in opposing whatever furthers the gospel. He works to obstruct the personal fellowship of believers. Satan hindered Paul. We know he tried to hinder Jesus of Nazareth. We know that he walks about as a roaring lion, seeking whom he may devour.

Paul says further:

> For what is our hope, or joy, or crown of rejoicing? Are not even ye in the presence of our Lord Jesus Christ at his coming (1 Thess. 2:19)?

Paul's greatest joy was in the believers he had won to the Lord. The treasure of many parents is children who believe in the Lord. And the treasure of many a pastor is the persons whom he has led to the Lord. Those are the ones he loves to think about; they will be his crown of rejoicing when he comes into the presence of the Lord Jesus Christ.

Notice the full name of the one who is coming: the Lord Jesus Christ. Will we recognize anyone at His coming? Paul expected to recognize persons that he had won. I have the same expectation that Paul had; I hope to see those whom I may have helped.

> For ye are our glory and joy (1 Thess. 2:20).

Witnessing for Christ at any time is like sowing seed. The harvest is faith in the people to whom we talk and before whom we walk—faith that leads to eternal life. Many experiences can distress and harass the believer, the witness; but the result of the witnessing, the souls won, are the glory and joy, the crown of every believer.

There is an important truth here. Consider what the apostle Paul is really saying when he tells the Thessalonians, "I wanted to come to see you that I might be blessed, but I was hindered. I labored abundantly because I hoped to be able to get there, but Satan hindered us."

The first testimony that makes an impression on a child is that of the parents. The way the parents act toward God, toward other people, and toward those in authority is a witness to the children. Parents are actually ministering to them, sharing with them the truth as it is in the Lord Jesus Christ. This is the sort of situation Satan will try to disturb.

When parents realize that things are happening to interfere with their testimony, they can be provoked to hasty words and become irritable. They are not wrong to think that Satan has something to do with this. But parents can remember that God is on their side. They can turn to the Lord and ask His help in the way they live and walk and talk, right in their own home.

FIRST THESSALONIANS
Chapter 3

† † †

NEW BELIEVERS SHOULD EXPECT
TO HAVE TROUBLE
(1 Thess. 3:1–3)

Do you realize that when a person becomes a believer in Christ he is bound to have trouble?

> Wherefore when we could no longer forbear, we thought it good to be left at Athens alone; and sent Timotheus our brother, and minister of God, and our fellowlabourer in the gospel of Christ, to establish you, and to comfort you concerning your faith (1 Thess. 3:1–2).

Paul evidently had great concern for the believers in Thessalonica. We know that he was anxious to see them and had tried very hard to get there. This was apparently not only for his own joy—which would have been great—but also that he might reassure them and strengthen them to endure in their faith in the Lord. When he could still not manage to get to them, the urgency of their situation moved him to send Timothy. This meant that Paul would be left alone in Athens, which was both distressing and weakening to him.

In sending Timothy, Paul showed the confidence that he had in this young preacher whom he looked upon as his own spiritual son, although here he calls him his brother. In writing to Timothy, Paul called him "my own son in the faith." Timothy was a child of God even as Paul was a child of God, and he was Paul's equal in service. Paul was a servant of God, a minister of God; and Timothy was also a minister of God. Timothy stood in his own strength as a servant of God, and

Paul wanted him to go and have fellowship with them and minister unto them.

"Our fellowlabourer in the gospel of Christ." Timothy was a fellow laborer in the gospel with Paul; they were sharing together, praying together, helping each other. It is wonderful to have fellowship in the service of the Lord. It is marvelous when, in a home, both husband and wife are believers who want to serve God, who work together in their concern for their children, and worship together in the church. Paul sent his fellow laborer, Timothy, to the Thessalonians "to establish you": to strengthen the believers by encouraging them to become more deeply rooted in the promises of God. A believer in Christ is one who is confident because of God's promises in Christ, one who is inspired to serve because God's grace is at work in him.

In his epistle to the Romans Paul wrote:

> For I long to see you, that I may impart unto you some spiritual gift, to the end ye may be established; that is, that I may be comforted together with you by the mutual faith both of you and me (Rom. 1:11–12).

He was eager to share the gospel with them so that they might be strengthened in it.

Timothy had experienced some spiritual truths that could comfort the Thessalonians. So Paul sent Timothy to them that all might be comforted and established in their mutual faith. This demonstrates how very important it is to be well acquainted with one's minister. It would be a blessing if you knew your preacher personally and he knew you, so that together you could strengthen each other.

> That no man should be moved by these afflictions: for yourselves know that we are appointed thereunto (1 Thess. 3:3).

The troubles a believer has that are related to his faith may include personal opposition to his witness. Perhaps someone takes exception to his testifying for the Lord Jesus Christ— someone in his home, or even in a Bible class. Paul told these believers not to be disturbed by those who opposed their testimony. For afflictions actually confirm the authenticity of a witness.

John Wesley, on one occasion when he had had no rotten eggs thrown at him for several days, wondered in his diary whether he had failed to preach the gospel. He expected persecution.

Afflictions lose their power when we consider their source, but they are still burdensome. Even though the believer knows they stem from unbelief, even though he realizes that people are criticizing him because they have no faith themselves, the criticism is still exhausting. Afflicted believers need to be established and comforted, and they will be by sincere, sound gospel preaching. All of us might wish that some Paul would send some Timothy to our church, to talk to us about the gospel and strengthen us in our faith for the sake of the Lord Jesus Christ.

AN EVANGELIST IS CONCERNED THAT HIS CONVERTS STAND TRUE
(1 Thess. 3:4–8)

Can you understand why a minister is strengthened when his converts are strong in faith?

> For verily, when we were with you, we told you before that we should suffer tribulation; even as it came to pass, and ye know. For this cause, when I could no longer forbear, I sent to know your faith, lest by some means the tempter have tempted you, and our labour be in vain (1 Thess. 3:4–5).

Paul had warned his converts in Thessalonica that they could expect trouble when they professed their faith. His warning had come to pass. For the truth is that open witnessing for Jesus Christ will often arouse opposition. Sometimes a person can witness for the Lord Jesus Christ in an obnoxious way. That brings opposition from anyone. But occasionally— even if one is careful in one's conduct, humble and meek in one's approach—people will still react by being unpleasant. It can even happen in church or at home.

Opposition is not always limited to words. Enemies of various kinds will often harass a person. Being warned enabled the Thessalonians to face opposition more confidently, because they were then prepared for it when it came.

Faith is something that must continue to grow. Even though it can begin in a moment, it cannot be "done" once and for all. Faith is not always strong. Knowing this, Paul feared that the Thessalonians might have been tempted by Satan.

Sometimes Satan tempts believers to doubt that there is a God, or that Jesus Christ is the Son of God. Such doubts interfere with the basis of their faith. But there are other ways Satan can get to believers. He may suggest that they doubt the Scriptures, or tempt them to make their own plans and leave God out. He may tempt them to think that because they have been believers for years they are good enough to please God just the way they are. Believers may figure that God is not going to judge them anyway; so they may relax and do what they please, without realizing that they have fallen into Satan's trap.

Once believers feel that they are strong enough and good enough in themselves, they may become proud. If that happens they will begin trusting in themselves and in all of that they will be moving away from God.

If this had happened at Thessalonica, Paul would have felt that his labor had been in vain. For what he had labored to show those people was that their salvation depended upon God. If they had now turned to some other way, Paul would have missed his purpose.

> But now when Timotheus came from you unto us, and brought us good tidings of your faith and charity, and that ye have good remembrance of us always, desiring greatly to see us, as we also to see you: therefore, brethren, we were comforted over you in all our affliction and distress by your faith (1 Thess. 3:6–7).

That is a remarkable statement. Paul testifies that he was comforted in his own affliction and distress by the faith of the Thessalonians. Just knowing that they believed strengthened him so much that he was able to endure his own circumstances. Paul had sent Timothy to check on conditions among the Thessalonians, and now he was blessed to hear the report of their faith and charity.

Sometimes we group the words "faith" and "charity" together without realizing their significance. Faith is the heart's attitude toward God; charity is the heart's attitude toward others. God does not need anything: I can only bring my devotion to Him. But people often need my charity.

The Thessalonians had the grace of God in them, and they demonstrated it in both their attitude toward God and their attitude toward other people. Their attitude toward God was faith in Him, and their attitude toward others was charitableness. Those two things had not changed since Paul had seen them, and when he heard this he rejoiced. For continuing to trust the grace of God in faith, and continuing to be charitable to all in love, are signs of spiritual health and vigor.

The Thessalonians also fondly remembered Paul and his ministry, "desiring greatly to see us, as we also to see you." Something very important takes place when believers get together. The hunger for this communion, the inward desire to be with other believers, is a healthy sign.

Paul added a final word:

> For now we live, if ye stand fast in the Lord (1 Thess. 3:8).

It is easy to understand that we live well, with a clear heart and mind, if we stand fast in the Lord. Paul derived strength to continue in his own ministry from the evidence of the continuing faith and charity of his converts.

All through this epistle we can sense the importance of fellowship—not just at church, but even in our own homes. If believing people share together, they will grow in the things of the Lord.

A PASTOR THANKS GOD FOR BELIEVING CHURCH MEMBERS
(1 Thess. 3:9–10)

Do you have any idea what a pastor asks for when he prays for his people?

> For what thanks can we render to God again for you, for all the joy wherewith we joy for your sakes before our God; night and day praying exceedingly that we might see your face, and might perfect that which is lacking in your faith (1 Thess. 3:9–10)?

These words simply tell us that Paul thanked God for the believers.

Becoming a believer is not a matter of human achievement; it is a matter of God giving a person the grace to believe. When someone really puts his or her trust in God, you can thank God for giving that kind of grace to that person.

Paul knew that he had done nothing to produce the Thessalonians' faith. He had no inclination to feel proud about them, for he was aware that everything that was happening in them was from God. Now he would rejoice in their forgiveness, and in the new nature that God had given them. He would rejoice in their joy in the Lord because God had enabled them to rejoice in Him.

When Paul wrote of "night and day praying exceedingly that we might see your face, and might perfect that which is lacking in your faith," he was indicating that he prayed at all times. It is humbling to read this about a great and busy man like Paul; he was exceedingly faithful in such matters.

Prayer is more than simply requesting or petitioning. Often we have the feeling that prayer is something like shopping at a bargain counter: we need something, and we hope we can get it without too much trouble or expense. But that is a very shallow view. Prayer includes praise and adoration, as well as thanksgiving. We approach God in a worshipful manner and with appreciation for what He has done. We praise God for His kindness to us when we do not deserve it.

Paul prayed often about the Thessalonians, thanking God for them. His first request was that he might see them face to face. Personal fellowship with other believers was of primary importance to him, and this should also be the case with us; it strengthens the heart.

Paul wanted to be sure that the faith of these people would be complete. For a person may believe in the Lord Jesus Christ without appreciating all that is available in Him. One may believe that He will forgive, and that He will save the soul. That is true: He will. But there is more: Christ will live in the soul, helping that person to carry life's burdens. This is the blessing Paul wanted these believers to have.

Paul wanted the Thessalonian believers to increase and abound in love toward all. He hoped that they would willingly minister in both their homes and their community. Paul also prayed that they should be sanctified in conduct, abstaining from fornication and from defrauding one another. He wanted them to act in a manner consistent with their faith. Not only did he pray about this; he actually sent Timothy to check up on things, to make sure that nothing was lacking.

Paul did not demand things of these Thessalonians: he wanted to give them something. He wanted to make sure they received what God had planned for them.

It is wonderful to belong to a group of Christian people, and it is wonderful when the Lord Jesus Christ has His way in our hearts.

LOVE IS BASIC TO HOLINESS
(1 Thess. 3:11–13)

Can you understand how love abounding in the heart of a believer promotes holiness?

> Now God himself and our Father, and our Lord Jesus Christ, direct our way unto you. And the Lord make you to increase and abound in love one toward another, and toward all men, even as we do toward you: to the end he may stablish your hearts unblameable in holiness before God, even our Father, at the coming of our Lord Jesus Christ with all his saints (1 Thess. 3:11–13).

In the course of his letter, Paul had told these believers that he longed to see them. He had tried to get to their section of the country in order to have fellowship with them, but Satan had hindered him. He does not tell the Thessalonians just what he will do to make sure he gets there; he wants God to "direct our way unto you." In other words, he is trusting God to make this possible. He accuses no one, and he takes no blame for having failed to do it until now. But this time he wants to get there.

Paul links together "God himself and our Father, and our Lord Jesus Christ." When he writes "God himself," Paul includes everything that has to do with providence. When he writes "and our Father," Paul refers to fellowship with God that would actually influence his own heart and mind. Thus, having communion with God as Father, he would be guided by "our Lord Jesus Christ." In any decision he needed to make, the presence of the Lord Jesus Christ would guide him.

Paul wanted to see these believers personally, and he had a feeling that if God took a hand, everything he did would work toward that end. So this was actually a prayer, a petition. He expected that God would bring His will to pass, but that his own desires would have a part in it. Apparently Paul counted on God the Father and His Son, the Lord Jesus Christ, to direct his course of action. If God did that, Satan could not thwart him.

In verse 12 Paul prayed, "And the Lord make you to increase and abound in love one toward another, and toward all men, even as we do toward you." Here he drew attention to the one thing he wanted for these people above all else.

Love is not generated by human will. It is not promoted by someone admonishing the believer to make sure he cares for people. Love increases and abounds in the heart by the grace of God. Paul does not put the burden upon the Thessalonians; he does not say, "make sure that you do." He says, "The Lord make sure."

God makes love increase and abound in the heart, so that it actually springs up into everlasting life. Love is always directed toward some person or thing. It is an action, a movement toward—not merely a feeling. Love is present when a person does something for others.

Electricity is very much like love. A person may know that the power that makes the lights burn and causes the refrigerator to operate comes into the house through electric wires. But unless he uses that electricity and turns it on, none will come. All the potential may be there. But if someone does not use it, no power at all comes through. Even so, love toward others must be exercised. When it is used, it will grow accordingly.

"To the end he may stablish your hearts unblameable in holiness before God" brings to mind a very practical truth. Everyone would like to feel that by the blessing and help of God they can be holy in His presence. We are told that "without holiness no man shall see the Lord," and we do want to see Him. Although we may be self-conscious about it, we all pray that by the grace of God holiness may develop. Here Paul has pointed out that this will happen as a result of abounding love. Paul wants the Lord to make believers increase and abound in love "to the end that he may stablish your hearts unblameable in holiness." And that is how it will be, "before God, even our Father, at the coming of our Lord Jesus Christ with all his saints." Here Paul refers to the Judgment Day when things will actually be identified for what they are.

There is no such thing as a believer having fellowship with God without having love in his heart. No believer will have any kind of association with God apart from the love he has toward other believers and toward all people.

The believer wants to do good to others if he can; he wants to help them if he can. He wants to increase their benefits and their blessings. This concern will actually develop in him as love abounds. When it develops in him, it will make him unblamable in holiness: he will be totally committed to seeking God's favor, totally committed to pleasing God.

If the believer is to be totally committed to God, God must work in his heart to will and to do of His good pleasure. John wrote, "God is love," and God must be the origin or source of any love the believer has toward God, other believers, and all other people. The believer's love toward God will be demonstrated in doing what God wants him to do; the believer's love toward fellow believers will be demonstrated in seeking their welfare. The believer's love toward others will include seeking to show them the gospel so that they might be saved.

FIRST THESSALONIANS
Chapter 4

† † †

THE CONTINUING CONCERN
OF A TRUE PASTOR
(1 Thess. 4:1)

Do you think a true pastor should ever be content with the state of his people?

> Furthermore then we beseech you, brethren, and exhort you by the Lord Jesus, that as ye have received of us how ye ought to walk and to please God, so ye would abound more and more (1 Thess. 4:1).

After Paul had told the Thessalonian believers of his concern for their faith, and of how he had rejoiced to get Timothy's report that they truly believed the gospel and abounded in love toward God, other believers, and all other people, he begged and exhorted them to abound still more. He wanted them to keep it going.

What has the apostle said in the first three chapters of this epistle? Paul has talked about their receiving the Word of God in much affliction and with joy of the Holy Spirit. When they heard Paul's preaching, they received it, even though it involved them in affliction. From other people they encountered ridicule and sarcasm. But believing the truth as it is in Christ Jesus had filled them with joy.

Their testimony had gone far and wide; everywhere people were talking about their faith in God.

These people had turned from idols to serve the living God. We may think that idols were only a problem in ancient times, but we must still reckon with them in the here and now.

Naturally we all make certain plans and have certain goals. We hope that what we do today will be good, and as we look ahead, we wonder how everything will turn out. We start to anticipate the results of what we have been doing. But that can become an end in itself. We can get so interested in what we are doing that we forget to be interested in God. We can begin to feel that we are running our own lives. That would be a mistake: we need to keep our eyes fixed upon God.

A believer should turn to God for assurance and joy. The Thessalonians turned away from the works of their hands and the things of the world to God, looking to Him for their assurance and joy.

Serving the living and true God requires being reverent, having no other gods before Him; being respectful, honoring one's father and mother; having regard for others; and showing charity to the poor. Furthermore, if I am a believer, the world should be able to tell by my actions that I expect the Son of God to return from heaven.

In 1 Thessalonians 2:12 Paul urged believers to walk worthy of God. To understand what this involves, we may note an appropriate passage of Scripture:

> I therefore, the prisoner of the Lord, beseech you that ye walk worthy of the vocation wherewith ye are called, with all lowliness and meekness, with longsuffering, forbearing one another in love; endeavouring to keep the unity of the Spirit in the bond of peace (Eph. 4:1–3).

Paul went on to say that they had received his preaching not as if it were the word of human beings, but as the very Word of God; and that they had become followers of the churches of God in Judea. Timothy brought good tidings of their faith and charity, which had led them to love one another and to love God, and to be gracious to all people.

Paul referred to this when he wrote, "Furthermore then we beseech you, brethren, and exhort you by the Lord Jesus, that as ye have received of us how ye ought to walk and to please God, so ye would abound more and more." Paul wanted them to keep it up and walk close to the Lord Jesus Christ.

SANCTIFICATION IS GOD'S WILL
FOR ALL BELIEVERS
(1 Thess. 4:2–6)

Do you realize that all believers have a responsibility to treat the body as the temple of God?

> For ye know what commandments we gave you by the Lord Jesus. For this is the will of God, even your sanctification, that ye should abstain from fornication: that every one of you should know how to possess his vessel in sanctification and honour; not in the lust of concupiscence, even as the Gentiles which know not God; that no man go beyond and defraud his brother in any matter: because that the Lord is the avenger of all such, as we also have forewarned you and testified (1 Thess. 4:2-6).

This Scripture has commonly been passed over because it is seen to refer primarily to immoral conduct. If a reader's conscience is clear where immorality is concerned he is likely to skip over it and move on. This passage does in fact refer to conduct that would be called immoral, but it refers to it in a much broader context than is commonly thought.

"What commandments we gave you." Paul had instructed his converts for living. He had explained to them what it would mean to walk in the Lord. That takes more than good intentions; it means counting on His presence and His control. In the Lord they would be led in new paths. They would have in them the Holy Spirit of God, who would activate the Lord's will in them.

Paul then wrote: "For this is the will of God, even your sanctification." For all believers at all times, under all situations, this is the will of God.

We are told that when Jesus of Nazareth was born, and again when He was baptized and identified before the world as the Son of God, almighty God said from heaven, "This is my beloved Son, in whom I am well pleased." When we look closely to see why God was well pleased, we remember that the Lord Jesus said, "The Son can do nothing of himself, but what he seeth the Father do" (John 5:19). He was completely obedient to His Father.

This is the Lord, the one in whom believers are to live. Living in Him, they are set apart unto God for His service. In

Paul's time there had been no concrete formulation of the doctrine of sanctification. The word "sanctification" meant simply "being set apart for a special purpose."

"That ye should abstain from fornication." This is usually taken to refer to sexual immorality. I am sure it does refer to that, but it means more. It includes any uncontrolled use of one's body for one's own satisfaction, which leads into immorality.

"That every one of you should know how to possess his vessel in sanctification and honor" means that everyone should know what is involved in self-control. "His vessel" means the container in which one lives. I do not think this refers so much to any particular part of the body as to the body as a whole. The believer is to know how to possess his body in sanctification—with controlled commitment, being set aside for a purpose. "And honor" means with special handling. The believer is to be careful in the way he acts.

"Not in the lust of concupiscence" is a phrase we do not ordinarily use. A good translation would be "not in the strong desire of self-indulgence."

"Even as the Gentiles which know not God." This does not mean that they have not heard of God, but that they do not esteem or appreciate God. They do not fear Him, and they do not try to obey Him; they go about their own affairs. Every believer should stay within his own rights and within what belongs to him, and not go beyond "and defraud his brother": he should not cheat his brother or take advantage of him in any matter.

The scope of this passage is broad, making it applicable to all intrapersonal relations and affairs. The guiding principle of self-control is respecting the rights of others, because "the Lord is the avenger of all such." He has a direct interest in every relationship, and He will not suffer anyone to be oppressed or robbed. Even those who do not know Him are His creatures. When anyone takes advantage of them, that person has offended God.

"As we also have forewarned you and testified." Paul had previously warned them about these truths. I think he is warning them against any misuse of the body, just as he had warned them that the mistreatment of others would be noted.

So we can say, with reference to this whole section, that sanctification is God's will for every Christian. It is designed to make the believer holy. Believers are to practice self-control, that they may do the will of God.

SELFISHNESS IS NOT AGAINST MAN, BUT AGAINST GOD
(1 Thess. 4:7–8)

Do you realize how very serious selfishness is?

> For God hath not called us into uncleanness, but unto holiness. He therefore that despiseth, despiseth not man, but God, who hath also given unto us his holy Spirit (1 Thess. 4:7–8).

The sphere in which the gospel operates in anybody who believes in and accepts the Lord Jesus Christ is that person's consciousness. It works in the mind, in the heart, and in the awareness. The gospel has more to say about attitudes than about actions, because actions are just outworkings of attitudes. Attitudes, in turn, are generally based upon values, upon what one prefers and what goals one cherishes.

The story of how sin emerged in this world in the Garden of Eden is well known. This happened when Adam and Eve began thinking about themselves rather than about God. The fruit of the Tree of the Knowledge of Good and Evil was good for food, pleasing to the eye, and a thing to be desired to make one wise. It aroused their self-interest. They committed sin when they disobeyed God and followed this self-interest. Because of Adam's and Eve's self-serving actions, the human heart became committed to self-serving. This is the character of sin to this day.

Because of sin, this inward proclivity on his part to do only what pleased himself, man was doomed. God could not tolerate sin.

The Good News is that Christ Jesus came to save the lost. He came to save those who in their selfishness had been condemned before God. He came to save them so that God could change them into His own likeness and make them His children.

One way God accomplishes this is through preaching, proclaiming the truth. Preaching the truth means far more than just setting it forth; it also means bringing the heart to believe it and receive it, as Paul is doing in this letter.

Paul goes on to say, "God hath not called us unto uncleanness." When would a garden be unclean? To answer, you might have to ask yourself what a weed is. Any plant growing out of place is a weed. The garden is unclean, then, when there are plants in it that are out of place. When is conduct unclean? When it has in it acts that are out of character, that do not belong; when the person does things and behaves in ways that are not the will of God. In general, it is when a person's actions are self-serving and not God-serving. Because the believer is not his own, and has been bought with a price, such behavior is improper and out of place; it is as unclean as an unwanted plant in a garden.

"But unto holiness." God has not called believers to be selfish, but to be completely yielded to Him. Remember that holiness actually means being one hundred percent committed to the Lord. This can be achieved anytime by anybody.

Sometimes people think that holiness is only acquired after a long time. But I do not think that is valid. Holiness is the result of being holy, of directing all of one's personality, interests, and energy toward pleasing God.

"He therefore that despiseth, despiseth not man, but God." How would a person despise the Scriptures? When he belittles them. A person whose whole attitude toward living is such that he does not do the will of God even when he knows what it is, is on dangerous ground. For the person who despises the Word of God is not despising human beings, but God.

If a person views the Bible as mere literature prepared by certain individuals who did the best they knew how, as nothing but pious mouthings of people who wanted to please God and therefore said everything in extravagant fashion, that person is despising Scripture. Or, if, after a person has heard the gospel, he is influenced by someone else who brings a message that is supposedly more complete or more perfect, that person has despised the Scripture that he heard.

Even in Paul's lifetime there were those who added to the message. When Paul preached the gospel in Galatia, some believed. Then others came along and said that everything Paul had preached may have been true, but they added to it. Paul told them emphatically that anybody who added to the Scripture he had preached was not speaking from God.

If people today for one reason or another do not use the Bible, what do they go by? What is left? Only human opinion, which is a trashy substitute. Scripture is not from man, but from God. Paul said that if people rely on the Bible, they rely on the very Word of God, and they will learn from it that holiness is what God wants. He wants the individual to deny himself and turn to Him. In return for that, God will give the believer Himself and all eternity.

THE MARKS OF BROTHERLY LOVE
(1 Thess. 4:9–12)

Do you have a clear idea of how brotherly love is manifested?

> But as touching brotherly love ye need not that I write unto you: for ye yourselves are taught of God to love one another. And indeed ye do it toward all the brethren which are in all Macedonia: but we beseech you, brethren, that ye increase more and more; and that ye study to be quiet, and to do your own business, and to work with your own hands, as we commanded you: that ye may walk honestly toward them that are without, and that ye may have lack of nothing. (1 Thess. 4:9–12).

One wonders how many people there are who realize what true brotherly love is. I sometimes get the feeling that people imagine brotherly love to be a kindly feeling that one has toward others. But to the apostle Paul, brotherly love was much more practical than that. Brotherly love is not derived from any human being. It is not something some smart person thought up and offered to us. Brotherly love is something that God teaches us as we can see from the verses we are considering.

How is it taught of God? We can grasp this more easily if we ponder its nature, as described in verse 9. Brotherly love is not merely a matter of attitude; it is a matter of action, of what one does.

Paul rejoiced in the report Timothy brought him that the Thessalonians prospered and abounded in love toward God and charity toward all people. The believers manifested that kind of behavior throughout the whole region. But Paul earnestly admonished them to make even greater progress.

What do we really mean when we talk of brotherly love? Paul wrote, "Ye need not that I write unto you." (You do not have any particular dependence upon my teaching, because God has taught you.) "For ye yourselves are taught of God to love one another. And indeed ye do it toward all the brethren which are in all Macedonia." (That is what Timothy has told him.)

"But we beseech you, brethren, that ye increase more and more; and that ye study to be quiet." In contrast to contention and quarreling, in contrast to being boisterous and loud, you should try to live quietly. This does not mean that you should be unconcerned, but neither does it mean that you should be flustered. It does not mean that you should be indifferent, but neither does it mean that you should be reckless.

How can one be aware of everything that is going on in the world and live quietly? How can one face everything and not be disturbed, see the dangers all around and not be upset? This is not easy, but it can be done if we try to see things from the Lord's perspective.

"And to do your own business." Can you understand that minding your own business is actually for the good of others? This is one aspect of brotherly love. "Love," in the biblical sense of the word, always implies doing something for the other person, seeking his welfare and happiness. When God loves us He does various things for us, and when we love God we praise Him.

"And to work with your own hands, as we commanded you." That is very specific. Do something that you have in your own hands to do. Be active. And why? "That ye may walk honestly toward them that are without, and that ye may have lack of nothing." You will not only win the respect of those outside the church; you will also earn your own keep.

It is wonderful to live among people who try to live quietly, who do not get needlessly aroused or make a big fuss about things, and who tend to their own business. This is not just good, common sense; it is also spiritual. It is what God wants the believer to do. When a believer lives this way, he is actually conducting himself in a manner that is to everyone's benefit.

THE CONFIDENT EXPECTATION
OF THE BELIEVER
(1 Thess. 4:13–14)

Can you understand why believers do not grieve as much as unbelievers when a loved one dies?

> But I would not have you to be ignorant, brethren, concerning them which are asleep, that ye sorrow not, even as others which have no hope. For if we believe that Jesus died and rose again, even so them also which sleep in Jesus will God bring with him (1 Thess. 4:13–14).

In his epistles Paul puts repeated emphasis on three traits. He indicates that a believer's life should be characterized by faith, love, and hope. Believers in Thessalonica manifested all three of these traits. Paul was concerned that they continue to grow in each category, and he sought to help them.

Where faith was concerned, Paul sent Timothy to check on and to aid the believers. Knowing that their faith might be tested and even shaken if they were having trouble, Paul told them that trouble was inevitable. Then he praised them for their performance and urged them to increase in devotion and in charity. After that he turned to the third characteristic: hope.

The hope of the believer in Christ is based on the Resurrection. Because he expects to live again, death is not so terrible.

Certainly death is an enemy, and there is nothing about it that we like. But it is not the final word.

Paul wrote to the Thessalonian believers, "I would not have you to be ignorant." When someone is expounding the Word of God, he should be impressing upon his hearers or readers what Christ has done, what Christ is now doing, and what Christ will do. If Paul had not told the Thessalonians what Christ would do, they would have been ignorant of it.

"Concerning them which are asleep." By this Paul simply means to say that death is not the last act. God's plan does not stop there. We might wonder why Paul uses the word "asleep." Some folks base a whole doctrine on this. (Perhaps you have heard someone talk about "soul sleep." But when Paul uses the word "sleep" in connection with death, he is never referring to the soul; he is referring to the body. It is the body that will fall asleep, and it is the body that will be awakened.

Paul uses the word "asleep" to emphasize that physical death is not final. When a person is asleep, he is unconscious of things: he does not know what is going on around him. But if he is only asleep, he can awaken and live again. When Paul writes about the body being asleep, he is thinking of the body being raised from the dead. He uses this figure of speech when he refers to believers who have died. They are "asleep" in the sense that their bodies are in the grave, but they will be awakened out of this state.

"That ye sorrow not, even as others which have no hope." Paul did not mean that believers would not grieve, nor did he say that they should not do so. Rather, he meant that they should not grieve as did those who had no hope.

There are people of whom it must be said that their outlook is confined to this world. For such people, when a loved one dies, he is gone for good. And when they think of dying themselves, they expect to be gone for good. For the believer it is not like that. For, while death is a state of unconsciousness, he knows he will wake up afterwards.

"For if we believe that Jesus died and rose again, even so them also which sleep in Jesus will God bring with him." There is a common notion that if there is a heaven, we will all be there; that if there is such a thing as a life hereafter, everybody will share it. But that goes beyond what the Scriptures say.

There is one parable in the Bible that very plainly tells us something about the future: the parable of the rich man and Lazarus (Luke 16:19–31). Both died: one went to heaven and the other went to hell. Both existed after death, which was not the end by any means. Christians should be clearly aware of the truth that only those who believe will be in heaven: "For if we believe that Jesus died and rose again, even so them also which sleep in Jesus will God bring with him."

The believer's faith in Christ's death and resurrection is basic and vital. No wonder the apostle Paul says

> That if thou shalt confess with thy mouth the Lord Jesus, and shalt believe in thine heart that God hath raised him from the dead, thou shalt be saved (Rom. 10:9).

In the above verse Paul uses the name "Jesus" by itself. He means Jesus of Nazareth in His physical body. It was the body of Jesus of Nazareth that died on the cross, and it was the body of Jesus of Nazareth that was raised from the dead. And just as surely as the body of Jesus of Nazareth rose from the dead, all believers shall rise from the dead.

This is the joy of the believer. He knows that those who sleep in Jesus will live, and that because of this, death is only temporary.

THE RETURN OF THE LORD
(1 Thess. 4:15–18)

Do you know what will happen when Christ comes again?

> For this we say unto you by the word of the Lord, that we which are alive and remain unto the coming of the Lord shall not prevent them which are asleep (1 Thess. 4:15).

The Lord will return. His teaching is so plain that there is no question about it. Remember the parables of the pounds and of the talents, in which He told of the absent master who would come back to judge his servants according to what they had done while he was gone? Then there is the parable of the ten virgins: all were expecting the Lord to come, but five of them did not think He was coming soon. You will also recall the parable of the sheep and the goats, which tells of the separation there will be when Christ returns.

There need be no doubt: the Lord is coming back. Jesus of Nazareth, who has been glorified as Jesus Christ, will return as Lord to judge the living and the dead.

In the foregoing passage, there is one word that I usually replace with a word that expresses the meaning more clearly. The King James Version reads, "we which are alive and remain unto the coming of the Lord shall not prevent them which are asleep." But the meaning of the word "prevent" has changed greatly since the King James Version was translated. This word has Latin roots: *pre*, meaning "before," and *venio*, meaning "to come." What "prevent" meant in earlier times was "to come before." Today we could use the word "precede," because that is exactly what it means.

"We which are alive and remain unto the coming of the Lord shall not *precede* them which are asleep." Those of us who are alive and remain (there will be a generation here on earth at the time the Lord returns) will not meet Christ first; He will first raise those who have fallen asleep in Jesus.

> For the Lord himself shall descend from heaven with a shout, with the voice of the archangel, and with the trump of God: and the dead in Christ shall rise first (1 Thess. 4:16).

Paul is not using the name "Jesus": he is saying "the Lord" shall return. Jesus of Nazareth is now glorified as both Lord and Christ, the Son of God, and He will come with authority. At the Ascension of the Lord Jesus Christ, when Jesus of Nazareth was taken up into heaven, the disciples were told:

> This same Jesus, which is taken up from you into heaven, shall so come in a like manner as ye have seen him go into heaven (Acts 1:11).

The emphasis was upon His body. The disciples saw Him go in His body, and people will see Him return in His body.

Sometimes people equate the coming of the Lord with His presence at a time of sorrow or great crisis. Or they think that the coming of the Lord will occur when one dies and He comes to receive one to Himself. But that is not what the Scripture says. The language Paul uses puts the matter beyond question: the Lord Himself shall descend from heaven. Right now He is physically present with God, and He will return physically to this world "with a shout, with the voice of the archangel, and with the trump of God."

No one knows what these sounds will be like. For now, all we know is that there will be some sudden, startling sounds, "and the dead in Christ shall rise first."

What is meant by "shall rise?" Even as Jesus Christ arose. He rose in the same body that was laid in the grave, but we should note that His risen body was somehow changed. So, too, the dead in Christ shall rise in the same bodies they had on earth. But these bodies will not be the same as they were before.

> Then we which are alive and remain shall be caught up together with them in the clouds, to meet the Lord in the air: and so shall we ever be with the Lord (1 Thess. 4:17).

After those who have fallen asleep in Jesus are raised from the dead in their resurrection bodies, the believers here on the earth at that time will be caught up.

Scripture gives us several pictures of this that we can keep in mind. Enoch in the Old Testament was a man who walked with God and "was not because God took him." The story of the prophet Elijah is even more vivid. Elijah went to a certain place with Elisha, and, while Elisha stood looking, Elijah was taken up into heaven. Likewise, Jesus of Nazareth, on the day of Ascension, was taken up into heaven in the presence of all the disciples.

I have pointed out that the body itself was changed. In the resurrection, the body will be different in its composition.

The body of Jesus of Nazareth went into the grave a natural body, but it came out of the grave a spiritual body. When it went into the grave it was composed of carbon, oxygen, hydrogen, nitrogen, and other various elements—earthly elements subject to time and space, and capable of being measured and weighed.

But when it was resurrected it was composed of spiritual elements—elements not limited by time and space, and not able to be measured and weighed.

At the coming of the Lord, those who are alive will be suddenly translated. We read in 1 Corinthians 15:51, "We shall not all sleep, but we shall all be changed." At the very moment when the Lord Jesus returns there will be something like an explosion, like spontaneous combustion, and suddenly the physical bodies of all believers will become spiritual in nature.

"Then we which are alive and remain shall be caught up together with them in the clouds, to meet the Lord in the air: and so shall we ever be with the Lord." That will be a permanent condition.

> Wherefore comfort one another with these words (1 Thess. 4:18).

The expectation of seeing the Lord, and one's family, face to face, is unique to the Christian faith. We trust that everyone reading these words will look up to the Lord and thank Him for the provision He has made for his or her salvation. If you have never accepted Christ, you can. And if you have been going along on your own, you do not need to. You can turn to the Lord. Receive Him, and He will receive you now and keep you forever.

FIRST THESSALONIANS
Chapter 5

† † †

THE COMING OF THE LORD
WILL BE UNEXPECTED
(1 Thess. 5:1–3)

Do you have any idea what we can know about the return of the Lord?

> But of the times and the seasons, brethren, ye have no need that I write unto you. For yourselves know perfectly that the day of the Lord so cometh as a thief in the night. For when they shall say, Peace and safety; then sudden destruction cometh upon them, as travail upon a woman with child; and they shall not escape (1 Thess. 5:1–3).

I have often been asked if I really expect Christ Jesus to return to this world in bodily form. I am always glad to make it very clear that I do. I expect Him to "come in like manner as ye have seen him go into heaven" (Acts 1:11). I believe in the Ascension of Jesus Christ. I believe He is in heaven now at the right hand of God, interceding for us. And I believe in His future return—His visible, personal, bodily return to this world—just as it is described in Scripture.

An interest in the Lord's return is normal. As a matter of fact, it is healthy; when it is lacking, there is something wrong. One of the assurances we have, as we handle the problems of daily life, is the knowledge that He is coming back.

We are by no means the only persons who have thought about this. Peter tells us that the Old Testament prophets were very much interested in the Second Coming of the Lord:

> Of which salvation the prophets have inquired and searched
> diligently, who prophesied of the grace that should come unto
> you: searching what, or what manner of time the Spirit of
> Christ which was in them did signify, when it testified be-
> forehand the sufferings of Christ, and the glory that should
> follow. Unto whom it was revealed, that not unto themselves,
> but unto us they did minister the things, which are now re-
> ported unto you by them that have preached the gospel unto
> you with the Holy Ghost sent down from heaven; which things
> the angels desire to look into (1 Peter 1:10–12).

In the Gospels we are told that when John the Baptist was
in prison, he sent a committee to talk to Jesus of Nazareth and
to ask, "Are you the one that is coming, or do we look for
another?"

The Jewish interpreters of Scripture questioned whether
there would be one Messiah or two Messiahs. Two things
were supposed to happen. According to Isaiah 53 the Messiah
would die, be "wounded for our transgressions, . . . bruised
for our iniquities." But according to Isaiah 11, the Messiah
would rule. The scholars did not see how one person could be
both: the Lamb who would die, and the King who would rule.

Jesus responded to the committee's question by inviting
them to watch Him. He healed the sick, opened the eyes of
the blind, and did various works of power that the Old Testament had said the King would do. He also sent word back to
John: "The blind receive their sight, and the lame walk, the
lepers are cleansed, and the deaf hear, the dead are raised up,
and the poor have the gospel preached to them" (Matt. 11:5).

After the Resurrection Jesus spent forty days with His
disciples, appearing on different occasions to teach them
about the kingdom of God. While He was with them the
disciples asked, "Lord, wilt thou at this time restore again the
kingdom to Israel?" (Acts 1:6).

I am reminded of the occasion in the Old Testament when
Absalom rebelled against his father, King David, forcing
David to flee for his life. After Absalom was defeated, David
waited until Absalom's backers showed a change of heart by
asking him to return. One of the people asked another, "Why
speak ye not a word of bringing the king back?" One has to ask
that question today throughout the Christian church.

Jesus of Nazareth answered this question about His coming
as Lord even before it was asked. He warned: "Watch there-

fore: for ye know not what hour your Lord doth come" (Matt.
24:42). He then told two sobering parables for emphasis. One
was about the unfaithful servant who did not expect the master to return that night, and who was judged because of his
abuse of fellow servants. The other was the story of the foolish
virgins who expected Him and even had lamps, but had no oil
in them. The Lord warned that "in such an hour as ye think
not the Son of man cometh" (Matt. 24:44). There will be no
buildup. The coming of the Lord will not be the consequence
of any natural process. "For when they shall say, Peace and
safety; then sudden destruction cometh upon them, as travail
upon a woman with child; and they shall not escape" (1 Thess.
5:3).

Peter gives a graphic portrayal of this whole matter in his
second epistle:

> Knowing this first, that there shall come in the last days scof-
> fers, walking after their own lusts, and saying, Where is the
> promise of his coming? For since the fathers fell asleep, all
> things continue as they were from the beginning of the crea-
> tion. For this they willingly are ignorant of, that by the word of
> God the heavens were of old, and the earth standing out of the
> water and in the water: whereby the world that then was, being
> overflowed with water, perished: but the heavens and the
> earth, which are now, by the same word are kept in store,
> reserved unto fire against the day of judgment and perdition of
> ungodly men. But, beloved, be not ignorant of this one thing,
> that one day is with the Lord as a thousand years, and a
> thousand years as one day. The Lord is not slack concerning his
> promise, as some men count slackness; but is longsuffering to
> us-ward, not willing that any should perish, but that all should
> come to repentance. But the day of the Lord will come as a
> thief in the night; in the which the heavens shall pass away with
> a great noise, and the elements shall melt with fervent heat,
> the earth also and the works that are therein shall be burned
> up. Seeing then that all these things shall be dissolved, what
> manner of persons ought ye to be in all holy conversation and
> godliness, looking for and hasting unto the coming of the day of
> God, wherein the heavens being on fire shall be dissolved, and
> the elements shall melt with fervent heat (2 Peter 3:3–12)?

So we turn our hearts toward God. We do not know when,
but we do know that He will send His Son, and that the Son
will come in flaming fire from heaven to judge the world and
to bring God's people into His presence.

THE ASSURANCE OF THE BELIEVER
(1 Thess. 5:4–5)

Do you understand why believers need not be in the dark about the future?

> But ye, brethren, are not in darkness, that that day should overtake you as a thief. Ye are all the children of light, and the children of the day: we are not of the night, nor of darkness (1 Thess. 5:4–5).

Ever since the Star of Bethlehem shone in the heavens and was afterwards seen and grasped, as it were, in the believer's heart, there has been a bright light shining in the future. That light is in heaven. The Bible tells us that believers are seated in the heavens. This is true even now in a spiritual sense. And I will remind you, there is no night there.

A song comes to mind: "In sorrow He is my comfort, in weakness He is my stay." Yes, in the darkest hour, His promises shine with heavenly light. In bereavement, He is with us. In love He comforts us. In loss, He is our assurance. Even if the whole world should pass away, He will never pass away.

Even if everyone else forsakes me, He will remain faithful. He has given His Word: "I will never leave thee nor forsake thee." When He said that, He knew who I was and who I would be. He knew how often I would disappoint Him, and how seldom I would do the things that I should. Yet this is the extent of His grace and mercy.

All this came back to me one night in California when I experienced my first earthquake. I awoke from a sound sleep to realize that my bed was shaking and moving across the floor. Outside, people were screaming in terror. The thought came to me that the bottom might just drop out, and my heart turned to water. But then it occurred to me that I should not worry, because one day I would leave this world, anyway. And I went back to sleep. In the midst of sudden shock I was given quietness and the peace that passes understanding.

Paul writes, "that that day should overtake you as a thief." Some day will be the last day; the end of all things will come. I think that will be true for the world as a whole, and I know it will be true for believers. That day does not need to overtake us as a thief would for we are the children of light.

"Ye are all the children of light, and the children of the day." God allows us to be here, and He watches over us. When we read that we are the children of the day, it means that we do not have to be in the dark about these matters.

The circumstances of my existence are known to me to some extent. When I read the Scriptures and when I look around, I can understand some of the reasons why I am here. Let me list some of the things that are true about me.

I was made by God; begotten by my parents; watched over and guided by Providence (He takes us by the hand and leads us); told by the gospel that Christ died for me; judged by God (I am like an open book to Him); saved by the grace of the Lord Jesus Christ.

God knows all people everywhere. He knows that "all have sinned and come short of the glory of God." It is the amazing and wonderful grace of this same God that "while we were yet sinners Christ died for us." And we praise Him for that.

Let me give you one thought that you can carry with you throughout this day and all the days to come: you are in God's hands and you are safe. Thank the Lord, and praise His holy name.

A BELIEVER'S MANNER OF LIFE IS DIFFERENT
(1 Thess. 5:6–8)

Can you understand why a believer acts differently from other people?

> Therefore let us not sleep, as do others; but let us watch and be sober. For they that sleep sleep in the night; and they that be drunken are drunken in the night. But let us, who are of the day, be sober, putting on the breastplate of faith and love; and for an helmet, the hope of salvation (1 Thess. 5:6–8).

When a minister of the gospel preaches to unbelievers, there is one message he wants to get across: you can be saved. When the unbeliever wonders what to do, he is told, "Only believe; it is all prepared for you. Come." But the minister of the gospel also has a message for believers. What is it? To believers he would say, as did the apostle Paul, "You can bear fruit. Only obey, follow on through." The person does not obey in order to be received, or in order to win something: he obeys because he has been received, and in order to achieve something for Christ's name's sake.

"Therefore (in view of everything that was in the first five verses of chapter 5) let us not sleep, as do others." When Paul uses the word "sleep" here, he is not referring to death as he did earlier in this epistle; he is referring to sleep as it is ordinarily understood. Sleep is a precious experience, and something we can thank God for. But it is not good for me to be sleeping when I should be working or watching. Why? Because when I sleep I am oblivious, unconcerned, and unattached.

"But let us watch and be sober." Not only should we watch the works of God and His grace within us; we should watch the fortunes of our loved ones and other people. For all are created by God. Let us have our eyes open, see how it is going with people, know what the situation is, and be sober.

The word "sober" does not refer to that state when a person is not intoxicated; here it means "serious-minded." Let us be alert to what goes on and take a responsible attitude toward it; let us be involved.

Paul then argues, "For they that sleep sleep in the night." Here again, when you sleep in the night it is without concern for others. You are without consciousness and you have no program of activity. How many people there are who, when it comes to their own spiritual condition or that of their loved ones, are in the night! They do not see; they do not do anything.

"And they that be drunken are drunken in the night." The effect of alcohol on the body is to unbalance the responses, to throw everything out of kilter. But does this passage refer only to people who drink alcohol? Oh, no. You can be drunk with all kinds of pleasure, whether it be in what you look at, in what you do, or in what you read or think. And if you are immersed in the affairs of this world with its riches and pleasures, you will be oblivious to the presence of God. You will be in barrenness where the Spirit of God is concerned.

Now look at the contrast in verse 8: "But let us, who are of the day. . . ." How can one be of the day? By being conscious, fully aware of what is going on. The person who is of the day is conscious of God, and of His works. The person who is of the day has also seen the cross of Calvary. He is conscious of the work of the Lord Jesus Christ and of the coming of the Holy Spirit at Pentecost.

"Be sober." Here we encounter the word "sober" again: serious-minded, living intently, wanting much to be done to the glory of God.

"Putting on the breastplate of faith and love." This is an act on our part, like putting on a coat or an apron. Where does the breastplate go? Over the breast. And what is in the breast? The heart. So a breastplate is a cover or protection for your emotions, something to keep them under control. You do not want to get overly upset about the bad things or overly optimistic about the good things; so you put on a breastplate of faith and love. Faith always points toward God, and love points toward everyone. Keep these things in mind, and your heart will be in order.

"And for an helmet, the hope of salvation." A helmet is something that you put on to protect your head—in this instance, to make sure you are thinking straight. If you would like to keep from being disturbed in your thinking, put on the hope of salvation as a helmet.

So we who are of the day guard our changeable emotions with faith toward God and love toward others. And where we ourselves are concerned, we thank God for salvation.

A BELIEVER'S LIFE IS PLANNED BY GOD
(1 Thess. 5:9–11)

Do you realize that every believer's future is planned for him by his heavenly Father?

> For God hath not appointed us to wrath, but to obtain salvation by our Lord Jesus Christ, who died for us, that, whether we wake or sleep, we should live together with him. Wherefore comfort yourselves together, and edify one another, even as also ye do (1 Thess. 5:9–11).

Planning for the future is normal. All of us are more or less inclined to do this; in fact, we might think that a person who is not looking toward the future is dull. Some people plan quite far ahead, selecting specific objectives and heading in that direction. Generally speaking, everybody has a plan for at least the next hour. We all hope that our plans will work out.

But a believer's outlook should be different. If you are a believer, and you approach all of life merely from the level of your own plans and dreams, you do not need to stay there.

The first thing a believer should realize is that the Lord has guided his life up to now. The Bible uses the word "Ebenezer," which is the Hebrew for "hitherto hath the Lord helped us." It is comforting to remember that I am where I am right now because Almighty God has brought certain things to pass. God is not responsible for everything I have done along the way, but He has overruled and controlled. I have wound up where I am because of Him.

We then become aware of a certain privilege the believer has: he can seek God's will about tomorrow. You may ask if I have plans. Yes, and many of them may not work out. However, it is comforting to know that even if all my plans do not work out, God's hand is in what happens to me. Always— even in sorrow, pain, trouble, and distress—He is having His way. That is why Paul could write, "In everything give thanks."

Now notice how Paul spells this out: "For God hath not appointed us to wrath." What does this mean? The word "wrath," as Paul uses it, refers to the consequence of doing evil. You can compare that word with the word "glory," which is the consequence of responding to the grace of God. The consequence of walking in God's will is God's blessing, which leads us into the glory that He has for us. We do not have to fear that our past will suddenly come up to haunt and thwart and crush us, that we will receive the consequences of our past mistakes. No, God has not appointed us to wrath.

We can be assured of this: that our sins have been carried away. We should rejoice in this and thank God for it. Some may fear that such confidence will set a person free to do whatever he pleases. But a believer will not please to do evil. When a person really believes that Christ Jesus died for him and has forgiven him, that God wants to be gracious toward him, and that he has the Holy Spirit of God in him, he will not want to do wrong.

"But to obtain salvation by our Lord Jesus Christ." The believer is to receive something worthwhile (salvation). The word "obtain" implies "by faith."

Paul then reminds the believers of the basic thrust of the gospel, speaking of Christ "who died for us, that, whether we wake or sleep, we should live together with him." When a believer thinks about the Lord Jesus Christ, he should start at Calvary. He should always remember that Christ died for him. That is the basis of his confidence, the assurance of his blessing. It is at that point that his salvation began.

When someone first becomes a believer, he rejoices that he is not going to hell. He will always be glad about this and will praise the Lord for it. Later on he will probably realize that salvation is much more than escaping hell. If God had not made him, he could never have gone to hell. But God both made him and sent His Son to die for him, that he might go to heaven. God had even more in mind: He wanted to bring that person to glory. So God had to forgive him, regenerate him, give him the Holy Spirit, work in him by His Spirit, surround him with His providence, take him by the hand, and—in spite of anything and everything he might do—bring him to Himself. That is the mind of God toward all who are in Christ Jesus.

"Wherefore comfort yourselves together, and edify one another, even as also ye do." When believers get together, they should be anxious to show one another the promises of God. Our fellowship together is most meaningful when we talk about what the Lord has done for us. When we think about His promises, we should try to strengthen one another in our mutual faith.

So the confidence of the believer is not based on his insight or intelligence, or on any effort he may put forth. His confidence is based upon the promises of God.

THE BELIEVER SHOULD HONOR HIS PASTOR
(1 Thess. 5:12–13)

Can you understand why a pastor should be highly respected by his congregation?

> And we beseech you, brethren, to know them which labour among you, and are over you in the Lord, and admonish you; and to esteem them very highly in love for their work's sake. And be at peace among yourselves (1 Thess. 5:12–13).

Paul wrote to the Thessalonians, in order to guide and encourage these believers in their spiritual life. He knew that it was very important for them to continue to believe in the Lord Jesus Christ and to have fellowship with other believers.

Paul was filled with joy when he heard of the faith and love of the believers in Thessalonica, and he wanted to see them face to face so that they all might be strengthened. He knew that faith and love do not just remain at the same level: they rise and fall. A believer's basis of confidence—Christ Jesus, who died for him—is always the same. But the faith and love in his heart need to be nurtured and encouraged.

There are two significant things that tend to increase a person's faith and love. One is fellowship with other believers. The other is a project of service in which he can exercise himself.

Faith and love in the heart are very much like the electricity that passes through a power line into your home. If on a certain day you used twice as much power as you did the day before, the power line would not be twice as thick or twice as long. There would be no difference in its appearance at all.

What then governs the flow of electricity? Is it the capacity of the generator that supplies the electricity to your house? No, that is not it. What actually determines the amount of electricity flowing into your house is the number of appliances you are using. The more you turn on, the more power comes through.

This is also how it is in our spiritual lives. We have as much power—as much faith and love—as we are willing to use. The more we use, the more we get.

In this vein, let us consider the matter of fellowship, of personal contact with other believers. Because he recognized the importance of right attitudes toward others, Paul was concerned that the Thessalonian believers get together for fellowship. He knew such gatherings would do much to encourage respect toward those who were in authority, regard for those who were fellows, and relief for those who were poor and needy.

The same principle applies to communal prayer. A believer will pray more if he goes to prayer meetings. Even if there is no longer a Wednesday night prayer meeting in the congregation, chances are that there are active prayer groups. The believer will be stronger if he takes part in one.

This is also true regarding projects of service. The believer will prosper as he cooperates with other believers in visitation or in a work detail at the church, or as he guides the efforts of church or community charity projects.

"To know them which labor among you, and are over you in the Lord, and admonish you." Here, the word "know" means "to esteem, to highly regard." In other words, the believer should respect the preacher.

When I first began my ministry, I keenly felt the responsibility of proclaiming the Word of God. I realized that I was not worthy to do it, but I also knew that I was to be God's spokesman to the people. Sometimes I was not very wise, and I became aware of the resentment my scoldings aroused. But there was one man in that congregation, an older man, whom I remember with appreciation. Even after I did (in my estimation) some of my poorest jobs of preaching, he would always come along with a big smile, lay his long arm across my shoulder and, pumping my right arm, say, "That's good preaching, son." I knew it was not good preaching, but that man said so every time. He made a better preacher out of me.

There were days when I would be ready to unburden my heart in a bitter comment to the congregation. Then I would remember that man who always told me that I was "all right," and I would find myself softening my remarks on his account. Will you remember that where your preacher is concerned? You may be fortunate enough to have a pastor who never requires a boost, but he will always appreciate your help even so. And if you are ever tempted to criticize him, remember that David—when he was a fugitive from Saul, who was trying to kill him—could have killed Saul. But David told his fellow soldier that he would not raise a hand against the Lord's anointed.

"And to esteem them very highly in love for their work's sake. And be at peace among yourselves." There is an old saying, A church's quarrel is the devil's picnic. Never let yourself get involved in a situation where church members are quarreling.

If you think your pastor is unfit, pray for him. If he is unable to handle his position, pray for him. If he is not living right, see to it that you live right, and pray for him. And keep this in mind: God knows everything you know, and even more.

A BELIEVER IS TO BE GRACIOUS TO EVERYBODY
(*1 Thess. 5:14–17*)

Can you understand why a believer should have sincere good will toward everybody?

> Now we exhort you, brethren, warn them that are unruly, comfort the feebleminded, support the weak, be patient toward all men. See that none render evil for evil unto any man; but ever follow that which is good, both among yourselves, and to all men. Rejoice evermore. Pray without ceasing (1 Thess. 5:14–17).

Because a believer has faith in God, he can look upon all people with good will. However, I am not saying that he always will. For all believers are not equally mature in a spiritual sense. Even after we become believers, the habits of the past may carry over, and our opinions be slow to change. One may, for example, feel suspicious of others; a person may have had experiences that cause him to feel that people are against him. This is unnecessary; a believer can have good will toward all people.

There is a reason for this. God made all people; He is over all. And in His providence He overrules all events, all things. The believer has no responsibility for things that have already happened or things that will happen. He is not to judge others.

The believer is indwelt by the Holy Spirit, who moves him to walk in the ways of the Lord. The more one walks with the Lord, he has thoughts of kindness, mercy, and grace toward people, looking upon each of them as a work of God for whom Christ died.

Believers are to "comfort the feebleminded." The word "comfort" is interesting: we are not to mistreat them or to be harsh with them.

"Support the weak." Some are not able to carry out their own desires. Not everybody who does wrong wants to do wrong. We need to support them.

"Be patient toward all men." This does not refer to believers only. ("Warning them" is for believers.)

"See that none render evil for evil unto any man." Some people are inclined to fight back; they want to retaliate if someone does them wrong. If you are a believer in the Lord Jesus Christ, do not do that.

"But ever follow that which is good, both among yourselves, and to all men." Does this mean that you are supposed to endorse everything that happens? Not at all. But let your part in it be for good. In anything you do, your aim is to be beneficial to other people.

"Rejoice evermore." In order to rejoice, you must first have joy; only then can you "rejoy." Have you had anything in your spiritual life to be joyful about? Did Christ Jesus forgive your sins? Then rejoice! Was it not a glad day when you learned Christ would not hold anything against you? Did you have joy? Then "rejoy." This means you should think it over, call it back to mind, bring it up over and over again.

"Pray without ceasing." That does not mean you should pray twenty-four hours a day, seven days a week. But it does mean you should keep it up day by day.

May the Lord help us in all these ways, that we may humbly yield ourselves to His guidance and be led in the ways of pleasantness and peace.

A BELIEVER NEEDS TO BE GUIDED
(1 Thess. 5:18–22)

If a person is a believer and knows that he is saved, does he need to have guidance for living?

> In every thing give thanks: for this is the will of God in Christ Jesus concerning you. Quench not the Spirit. Despise not prophesyings. Prove all things; hold fast that which is good. Abstain from all appearance of evil (1 Thess. 5:18–22).

We might ask ourselves why it is so important to give thanks to God. To be sure, God rules over everything; He is high and holy and almighty. But why is it important for me to give Him thanks? Giving thanks to God honors Him. When I thank God, I admit to myself that I did not do whatever I am thanking Him for: God did it. Giving thanks to the Lord is humbling. It causes me to remember that every day I am surrounded by God's good gifts—far more of them than I deserve.

Then again, thanksgiving encourages faith. If God has done all these things for me until now, what do you think He will do tomorrow? I can expect Him to do more of the same. This strengthens my faith. We should remember that thanks is one thing we can give to God. It may sound trite, but let me say this: I am the only one who can do it. If I do it, God receives it.

Does God want all this thanks only for Himself? No, He also wants it for His Son. God knows very well that the reason I am blessed is because Christ Jesus died for me. I have God's favor because the Lord Jesus Christ has reconciled me to God, and mediates between God and myself. I am blessed day by day because He died for me and prays for me.

It would appear from Scripture that God the Father wants the name of the Lord Jesus Christ to be glorified. If I had no other reason for giving thanks, it would be enough to do it so that the name of the Lord Jesus Christ should be exalted.

"Quench not the Spirit." This language suggests that the Spirit acts in our hearts like a fire. The Spirit will prompt me to act in line with God's will, to witness, and to pray. We can quench the inward prompting of the Spirit by not obeying. If the Spirit prompts me to pray, but I do something else first, I will be "throwing cold water" on the promptings of the Spirit. This is all too easy to do.

"Despise not prophesyings." When Paul used the word "prophesyings," I think he is referring to interpretation of Scripture. If you are in a Bible class or at church, and the meaning of a Scripture passage is opened up for you, or if you in reading the Bible have an inner prompting about some passage, you can be tempted to belittle it. Paul says, "despise not," do not belittle these interpretations that come to you.

"Prove all things; hold fast that which is good." The word "prove" means "test," or "check with Scripture." Test all things, even your own conduct. By their fruits you shall know them.

Finally we have this word: "Abstain from all appearance of evil." Do not even look like you are doing wrong; do not use the language that careless people use. You should even be careful about your dress and your companions. Remember, you belong to the Lord. You can honor Him by being sensitive about the ways in which you obey Him.

A BELIEVER CAN BE SURE
OF GOING TO HEAVEN
(1 Thess. 5:23–24)

Can you understand why the believer can be sure of going to heaven?

> And the very God of peace sanctify you wholly; and I pray God your whole spirit and soul and body be preserved blameless unto the coming of our Lord Jesus Christ. Faithful is he that calleth you, who also will do it (1 Thess. 5:23–24).

When I first became a believer, I rejoiced in the prospect of going to heaven. Part of that joy was a response to the fact that I was not going to hell. Thank the Lord! Let us who believe share the joy of this. We have a home to go to. In the Bible we are told that in the world we shall have tribulation; we cannot get through this world without trouble, sorrow, and grief.

It is the believer's joyous confidence that he is headed out of tribulation and chaos into peace. In this passage there is the promise that God is actually "the very God of peace." This does not just mean that we are to include God in our thoughts, and that that will give us a peaceful feeling; it is far more than that. The real, personal God is alive and active in our affairs. But in this life His way is not to stop all the trouble or to smooth out all the rough places. His way is to give us peace in the midst of trouble. He will give us quietness and confidence amid the confusion. He will build, as it were, a wall around us, and keep us in peace in spite of all the turmoil.

We do not worship an ideal, as such; our faith is not just an intellectual notion. Our trust is an active being: Someone who can and Someone who does. When we become aware of that, it humbles us. We are even now in the presence of God, and His hand is on everything; He will keep us in perfect peace if our minds are stayed upon Him.

First, He assures me that by His grace He forgives my sins. Not only does He forgive my sins; He also gives me an inward grace that enables me to stand up and to endure. The heavy weight of the storm will not beat me down, because He will shelter me. He is a Rock that is higher than I, and I am told to flee to that Rock and to rest in Him, to take shelter in Him.

Paul goes on to pray that this "very God of peace sanctify you wholly." God "preserves," which is a different way of saying He "saves." My soul and body will be saved "blameless unto the coming of our Lord Jesus Christ." Blameless does not mean that I never make a mistake, or that everything is perfect with me. But no blame is to be attached. God will make me acceptable "unto the coming of our Lord Jesus Christ."

Notice the full title Paul uses: it is not unto the coming of "Jesus," but unto the coming of "our Lord Jesus Christ." Jesus, who became incarnate; Christ, the chosen one of God who came to perform the service of salvation; and Lord, as He is now over all—King of Kings and Lord of all.

Paul then concludes: "Faithful is he that calleth you, who also will do it." Salvation is the work of God. I can depend upon it.

BELIEVERS ENJOY A BLESSED FELLOWSHIP
(1 Thess. 5:25–28)

Can you understand why believers feel differently toward one another than they do toward other persons?

> Brethren, pray for us. Greet all the brethren with a holy kiss. I charge you by the Lord that this epistle be read unto all the holy brethren. The grace of our Lord Jesus Christ be with you. Amen (1 Thess. 5:25–28).

Accepting Jesus Christ as Savior and Lord means opening the door to a new life style. Sometimes it is easy to forget that there are people who do not believe in the Lord Jesus Christ. Some of these people may appear to be stable and to live very self-confidently. Perhaps they are not happy about everything, but they take themselves and others as they are. It sometimes escapes us that such people may not have any feelings of loss or guilt; they do not know any better.

The unbeliever is alone, by himself or herself, whereas the believer is never alone. He is with the Lord. Not only is he with the Lord, but he is with other believers; he belongs to them also. These things are brought out as Paul comes to the close of his first letter to the Thessalonians.

"Brethren, pray for us." Paul is saying, "We belong to you; you belong to us; we all belong together. Share with us so that our common faith will be strong. That is what we want you to pray for." Let us never forget that the believer, the person the world calls a Christian, does not see things differently with his human eyes. It is in his heart and spirit that he is conscious of the reality and promises of God. And it is there that he commits himself to these promises. That is what we mean by faith. But faith is not something one is born with: faith is one's response to the revelation of God.

It is important to remember that one's faith may be stronger or weaker; it is very much like one's body in that it needs to be fed to be strong. To have a strong faith a person needs prayer. Other people need to pray for the believer as much as he needs to pray for himself, that faith may be strong and grace in effect, and that the Spirit may work in him to overcome the flesh. All of this is implied in "Brethren, pray for us."

"Greet all the brethren with a holy kiss." Let other believers know that you care for them. "All the brethren" means having no favorites. That involves personal discipline. I have known some believers with whom I found it difficult to be close. But I needed to overcome that barrier, to remember that they were mine and I was theirs. I should have greeted them with a holy kiss (which was, according to the social customs of that time, a gesture of affection). The form could have varied, but never the meaning. In my case a handshake would have been appropriate.

The apostle continues, "I charge you by the Lord that this epistle be read unto all the holy brethren." He meant that he would hold them personally responsible before the Lord for making sure that other believers heard the letter. They were to do this not because Paul asked them to, but because Christ Jesus had given Himself for them. Paul wanted to give everyone the chance to hear what he had written in this first epistle; they had every right to hear. The Lord was entitled to see the fullest result of His sacrifice. If they did as Paul directed, they would be stronger in faith and yield more to God. And that would mean more glory to the Lord Jesus Christ.

The apostle ends with this greeting: "The grace of our Lord Jesus Christ be with you." God's kindness and favor is to be extended toward all the believers in Thessalonica.

God does things for me that I do not deserve, and He enables me to respond to Him, to obey His will. Such obedience begins when I deny myself and agree to do what He wants me to do, even though I may not want to do it. All of this will follow because the grace of the Lord Jesus Christ is at work in my heart.

In this first epistle to the Thessalonians, Paul has set forth all that is involved in the gospel of the Lord Jesus Christ. If we draw nearer to Him, He will draw nearer to us. "Look unto me, and be ye saved, all the ends of the earth: for I am God, and there is none else" (Isa. 45:22).

SECOND THESSALONIANS

SECOND THESSALONIANS
Chapter 1

✝   ✝   ✝

TRUE BELIEVERS GROW IN RESPONSE TO THE GRACE OF GOD
(2 Thess. 1:1–5)

Can you understand why a true believer will have patience and faith in times of trouble?

> Paul, and Silvanus, and Timotheus, unto the church of the Thessalonians in God our Father and the Lord Jesus Christ: Grace unto you, and peace, from God our Father and the Lord Jesus Christ. We are bound to thank God always for you, brethren, as it is meet, because that your faith groweth exceedingly, and the charity of every one of you all toward each other aboundeth; so that we ourselves glory in you in the churches of God for your patience and faith in all your persecutions and tribulations that ye endure: which is a manifest token of the righteous judgment of God, that ye may be counted worthy of the kingdom of God, for which ye also suffer (2 Thess. 1:1–5).

In these verses Paul refers first to certain universal traits of believers, and then to some special traits that were indicative to him of God's grace in the hearts of these people.

You will notice that here again the traits of faith (toward God) and charity (toward one another) are mentioned. These traits are to be found in all persons who believe. Paul wrote that he was bound to thank God always for them because their faith was growing exceedingly and because "the charity of every one of you all toward each other aboundeth."

Faith comes by hearing, and hearing by the Word of God. So it follows that paying attention to the Bible should increase a person's faith. Peter wrote, "As newborn babes, desire the sincere milk of the word, that ye may grow thereby" (1 Peter 2:2). The more you understand the Scriptures and take them to heart, the more you will grow.

A believer should read the Bible and meditate upon it, trying to get a grasp of the events that are involved and the things that are being said. He should search the Scriptures for ideas and thoughts that will bear upon particular problems. As surely as the believer does this, his faith will grow and his love will abound.

Such faith is not just a matter of believing that Jesus Christ is the Son of God. Nor is it necessarily a matter of believing the content of Scripture more and more; one may believe it entirely to begin with. Faith is to be exercised as the believer lives. Is the prospect of living through this day threatening? Is he feeling discouraged? He should look up and listen, hear God's promises, and believe.

"And the charity of every one of you all toward each other aboundeth." A believer may feel very kindly toward folks who are some distance away, or people who lived a generation ago, or people who will live in the next generation. But what about his attitude toward those he lives with? What about good will toward his relatives and friendship with his neighbors? Is charity increasing in him? It could. We all recognize that people have different temperaments. Some are cheerful, while others are sulky. This may be their natural disposition. But a believer's charity toward others should not depend upon their disposition.

Charity in the believer comes from God. When Paul used the phrase "the charity of every one of you all," he was saying that charity is to be universal among believers. "Toward each other." This refers not only to the believers in one's own congregation, but to those in every denomination.

Paul then points to a second pair of traits that are special in nature and in origin: the Thessalonians' "patience and faith" in their particular situation in spite of unusually difficult circumstances. "Which is a manifest token of the righteous judgment of God." The fact that these people had been given the grace to endure trials justified God's righteous judgment in blessing them for their response to Him.

God does not confer his grace upon everyone. The Lord Jesus Christ said, "Give not that which is holy unto the dogs, neither cast ye your pearls before swine" (Matt. 7:6). I know that is a hard word, but there are people who do not pay any attention to God; He knows who they are, and He is not going to cast His pearls before them. If a person is not willing to respond, he will be turned away.

Who will be counted worthy of the kingdom of God? Those who are willing to respond. Why will they be counted worthy? Because of their patience and faith in difficult times. To be sure, salvation is not earned; it is a gift from God the Father, bought for us by the death of Jesus Christ, His Son.

THE LORD WILL DESTROY UNBELIEVERS AT HIS RETURN
(2 Thess. 1:6–9)

Can you understand that it is just for God to destroy the ungodly?

> Seeing it is a righteous thing with God to recompense tribulation to them that trouble you; and to you who are troubled rest with us, when the Lord Jesus shall be revealed from heaven with his mighty angels, in flaming fire taking vengeance on them that know not God, and that obey not the gospel of our Lord Jesus Christ: who shall be punished with everlasting destruction from the presence of the Lord, and from the glory of his power (2 Thess. 1:6–9).

It is common for those of us who think about these things to mistake God's long-suffering for slackness, and to think that because God has not done anything up to now, He does not really care. It is easy to think that, because the heavens appear to be silent in the face of all kinds of distress and trouble, God is indifferent. But the Scriptures tell us plainly that God is not mocked.

Death and destruction are rampant in this world, but there is one note of victory in it: "But God raised him from the dead" (Acts 13:30). Apart from the grace of God and the resurrection power of Christ, all creation faces death, the one invincible foe.

The Bible reveals that God holds all things in His hand. Even when there is trouble in this world, He is there. God will both hand out trouble and provide rest at the time of judgment: He will destroy the wicked and save those who believe in Him. These things will come to pass at the return of the Lord. It is about the latter that Paul is now writing.

In verses 6 to 9 we are dealing with something that is both sobering and unavoidable; it will definitely come to pass. Almighty God watches over all things. He can be patient and allow things to take what seems to be their natural course. But nothing happens in this world that He does not see and evaluate, and that He will not deal with.

"Seeing it is a righteous thing with God to recompense tribulation to them that trouble you." "Recompense" means "pay back," and "tribulation" means "trouble." Often we have the feeling that to be just God must be merciful. That is true: to be righteous in judgment, God will show mercy. However, there is another aspect of justice: God will not allow evil to go unpunished. And He will turn His back on those who turn their backs on Him. That is both fair and righteous.

"And to you who are troubled rest with us, when the Lord Jesus shall be revealed from heaven with his mighty angels." Generally speaking, the apostle Paul includes the title of Christ. But here he speaks of "the Lord Jesus," referring to Jesus of Nazareth in His glorified body. In order to understand this particular passage, it is important to remember that the Son of God is alive even though He is no longer Jesus of Nazareth as He walked the streets of Jerusalem. He is glorified, but He is the same person. He is now Lord over all, and He is at the right hand of the Father. But there will be a time when the Lord Jesus shall be revealed from heaven with His mighty angels.

When some people talk about the coming of the Lord, they give the impression that they think He might emerge among us. But when Jesus of Nazareth comes, He will come suddenly from heaven with His angels. He will come with power, "in flaming fire taking vengeance on them that know not God, and that obey not the gospel of our Lord Jesus Christ." These are not just words; they are an actual description of what will happen.

You will remember that I have pointed out to you that, in the Greek language, the word for "knowing" God connotes the idea of esteeming, appreciating, honoring Him. There are some people who do not esteem the God of the Bible, the God and Father of the Lord Jesus Christ, the God of Abraham, Isaac, and Jacob. There are some who do not respond; they do not heed the call of the gospel. A day is coming when almighty God will deal with such persons.

"From the presence of the Lord," which is heaven, "and from the glory of His power," which is the result of His grace, these people will be punished with everlasting destruction. That is a very sobering message, difficult to appreciate fully. If you should feel that it does not sound like other aspects of the gospel you have heard emphasized, you are right. I am talking about terrible destruction brought about by God almighty.

How easy it is for us to assume that God is other than the author of the universe. But He holds all things in His hands, and one day He will bring His will to pass with power in the coming of the Lord Jesus Christ.

SALVATION INCLUDES HEAVEN
(2 Thess. 1:10–12)

Can you see that salvation is not complete until the believer is in heaven with the Lord?

> When he shall come to be glorified in his saints, and to be admired in all them that believe (because our testimony among you was believed) in that day. Wherefore also we pray always for you, that our God would count you worthy of this calling, and fulfill all the good pleasure of his goodness, and the work of faith with power: that the name of our Lord Jesus Christ may be glorified in you, and ye in him, according to the grace of our God and the Lord Jesus Christ (2 Thess. 1:10–12).

In these verses the apostle Paul is talking about the expectation he has for the believers. How can a believer be worthy of this plan of God—that he should live forever in God's presence like the Lord Jesus Christ? He can be worthy if his response to God is genuine. God is not asking that person to do anything, but He is asking him to receive what He wants to give him. If the believer responds genuinely to the call of God, yielding himself to and following God, he can hear, "Well done, thou good and faithful servant."

A believer will be worthy if he is like the five wise virgins in the parable of the ten virgins who were waiting for the bridegroom. You will remember that the wise had oil in their lamps so that they would be ready to meet him; the foolish ones did not think he was coming back that night, so they had no oil in theirs. Because of their foolishness, they missed the wedding.

God's call is clear, gracious, and specific. He calls us to Himself, and we are to come. If we come, we will be counted worthy, and He will fulfill all the good pleasure of his goodness, and the work of faith with power." This means that God will carry out His salvation plan in the believer. If the believer has fallen asleep, he will be raised from the dead, and if he is still alive, he will be changed by the power of God. God will bring believing people into His presence, ready for Him forever, "That the name of our Lord Jesus Christ may be glorified in you."

When the believer is at last in the presence of God like the Lord Jesus Christ, the work of Christ will be finished, and in that sense He will be glorified. "He shall see the travail of his soul, and shall be satisfied" (Isa. 53:11). The work of God is not complete when I am forgiven or when it is settled that I will escape judgment. His whole program is not complete until I am brought into His presence, "according to the grace of our God and the Lord Jesus Christ." Actually, salvation is all of grace from start to finish.

So Paul has again reminded the Thessalonian believers of a remarkable truth: that God, by His grace, is undertaking to completely save all those who come to Him through the Lord Jesus Christ. He wants to enter our hearts and take us beyond the life of this world into His very presence—not only for the moment, but forever. For we belong entirely to Him.

SECOND THESSALONIANS
Chapter 2

† † †

THE IMMINENT RETURN OF CHRIST SHOULD NOT BE DISTURBING
(2 Thess. 2:1–4)

Do you know why the believer should not be disturbed at the prospect of the Lord's return?

> Now we beseech you, brethren, by the coming of our Lord Jesus Christ, and by our gathering together unto him, that ye be not soon shaken in mind, or be troubled, neither by spirit, nor by word, nor by letter as from us, as that the day of Christ is at hand. Let no man deceive you by any means: for that day shall not come, except there come a falling away first, and that man of sin be revealed, the son of perdition; who opposeth and exalteth himself above all that is called God, or that is worshipped; so that he as God sitteth in the temple of God, showing himself that he is God (2 Thess. 2:1–4).

It is very easy to be misled regarding the return of the Lord. One reason why this is so is because it has not happened yet, and any word we receive on it is incomplete. We cannot possibly imagine what it will be like; the above verses only hint at what will happen. Paul says, "Let no man deceive you by any means: for that day shall not come, except there come a falling away first, and that man of sin be revealed, the son of perdition." All we can say for sure about Christ's return is that certain things must happen first.

Again and again in church history, people have felt that the last events were taking place in their own generation. Christopher Columbus thought that the Lord would come in his lifetime. And because he had read in Isaiah that the message of God was to be taken to the islands of the sea before the end of time, he made his first trip—not to find a route to India, but to find the islands where there were people who needed to hear the gospel. That is also why Columbus made his second and third voyages. It has been said that by the time of his fourth voyage he was heartsick because people were using his discoveries to increase commerce instead of as an opportunity to take the gospel to the inhabitants of the West Indies. In one generation after another, people have felt that all the right signs were occurring and all the necessary conditions were being met. But Christ's return has not happened up to now.

Do not misunderstand me. I really believe the Lord's return will take place. But I do not believe that anybody will be able to anticipate it. The Lord Jesus said, "It is not for you to know the times or the seasons" (Acts 1:7).

We know that some things must happen first: for instance, the "falling away" to which Paul referred. There have been many times when people have thought, "This is the apostasy." Many Christians today think we are living in the time of apostasy. But what they are seeing is nothing new; people have been falling away from the Lord all during the history of the church.

There are those who feel sure that the "man of sin" will be someone with a real body. Even in our lifetime people have identified various leaders in Europe as the man of sin, but apparently they have not been correct. In his epistles John talks about a coming "antichrist," but he also says that there were antichrists in his time. In the latter case, the word "antichrist" simply refers to those who are opposed to the Lord Jesus Christ, and you will find them all around.

It is common to hear people say, "Christ may come tonight." That would mean that the conditions that have been outlined here have been met, and we do not know that for sure. The Bible's teaching on this has never been convincingly interpreted. But the prediction is plain: antichrist will come. Speaking about this Paul says in verse 4, "Who opposeth and exalteth himself above all that is called God, or that is worshipped; so that he as God sitteth in the temple of God, showing himself that he is God."

Let me humbly express, if I may, some of my thoughts in this connection. Where is the temple of God today, and what do we mean by the temple of God? Every believer knows that Scripture says that his body is the temple of the Holy Spirit. In Ephesians 2:21–22, the church is spoken of as being built together as a dwelling for God.

What Paul has written implies that a time will come when human beings will see themselves as having the authority God has. The full spiritual significance of this is unclear. But whenever I see people blandly ignoring God and thinking that they can manage their own lives, I am reminded that the spirit of antichrist prevails and has prevailed all through these latter days, since the time of the Lord Jesus and since Pentecost. I believe that the days will get worse, that there will be a ripening. However, this leads me to remember that Christ will come at an hour when we are not expecting Him.

Scripture makes it clear that one of these days will be the last day. While the time of the Lord's coming may not be certain, we can know that man is destined to die once. We may not be here until He comes, but we believe that we are going to be with Him. And I pray that the Lord will find us all ready when He comes in the air to take us home.

THE WORST IS YET TO COME
(2 Thess. 2:5–10)

Do you realize that things could be worse than they are?

Remember ye not, that, when I was yet with you, I told you these things? And now ye know what withholdeth that he might be revealed in his time. For the mystery of iniquity doth already work: only he who now letteth will let, until he be taken out of the way. And then shall that Wicked be revealed, whom the Lord shall consume with the spirit of his mouth, and shall destroy with the brightness of his coming: even him, whose coming is after the workings of Satan with all power and signs and lying wonders, and with all deceivableness of unrighteousness in them that perish; because they received not the love of the truth, that they might be saved (2 Thess. 2:5–10).

When Paul asks, "Remember ye not, that, when I was yet with you, I told you these things?" he is indicating that he had already warned the people that trouble was coming. World conditions were bad in Paul's time, as we read in Romans 1; and Paul knew that they would get worse, as we read in 2 Timothy 3. In the above passage Paul predicts that the revelation of evil will continue to worsen until it reaches a climax. The Revelation of John has the most to say about this, but we also find it addressed in 2 Thessalonians 5.

"And now ye know what withholdeth that he might be revealed in his time. For the mystery of iniquity doth already work; only he who now letteth will let, until he be taken out of the way." At the time the King James translation was made, the word "let" meant "hinder." Although evil was working widely in Paul's time, there was a restraining power that was in effect; things were not yet as bad as they could be.

You will remember that in the Sermon on the Mount the Lord Jesus said, "Ye are the light of the world." Light dispels darkness. He also said, "Ye are the salt of the earth." In those days salt was used to preserve meat. Wherever there are believers who let their light shine, the darkness is hindered just that much. And wherever believers walk faithfully, letting their works show, their faith and trust in God act like salt and restrain the activities of the wicked.

At present God Himself is also exercising restraint on the forces of evil. But a day is coming when He will restrain them no longer.

"And then shall that Wicked be revealed, whom the Lord shall consume with the spirit of his mouth, and shall destroy with the brightness of his coming." Paul seems to indicate that a "wicked one" will come. That wicked one might take the shape of a person commonly called the man of sin. In any case, things will get worse just before the world ends. Evil influences will be rampant during this time.

As I look about me, I would find it easy to think that we are in that time now. Today we see people who not only do evil, but who have no conscience about it. Not only do they disregard God; they feel smart about doing so.

"Even him (this man of sin), whose coming is after the working of Satan with all power and signs and lying wonders."

This is very sobering to read. Sometimes we think that great deeds are sure evidence that God is at work. No, not necessarily. Works of power are not always good. Things that look impressive on the surface are not always from God.

"With all deceivableness of unrighteousness in them that perish; because they received not the love of the truth, that they might be saved." The wicked one will have power to imitate things that are from God. There will be deceitful signs and miracles and wonders that are actually worked by the evil one. So we must say that as impressive as miracles are, they are not the best evidence of God's power. For God's power can be imitated.

We often feel that an all-powerful God should continue promoting good on earth indefinitely. But let me remind you that God did the one really important thing so far as this world is concerned when He gave His Son to die for sinners. No person has greater love than the one who lays down his life for his friends, and that is what the Lord Jesus did. That will be God's answer to the wickedness that in time will be rampant in the world.

Humbly we turn our hearts to God and ask Him to keep us. And we urge one another to draw as close to the Lord as possible. For as this Scripture passage plainly shows, there is an evil power lurking in the shadows.

UNBELIEVERS ARE DOOMED TO DESTRUCTION
(2 Thess. 2:11–14)

Do you know that the Bible reveals that there will be a great separation of all mankind?

> And for this cause God shall send them strong delusion, that they should believe a lie: that they all might be damned who believed not the truth, but had pleasure in unrighteousness (2 Thess. 2:11–12).

This is as plain as words can express it.

Throughout the Scriptures we are warned of coming judgment. The parable of the wheat and the tares is well known. The Lord does not separate them while they are growing, but they will be separated in the harvest. A similar parable is the parable of the sheep and the goats: the two may be together now, but they will not remain that way.

Jesus of Nazareth taught that the master will come back to judge His servants. This is the truth; there is no other outlook.

Everyone who preaches the gospel loves to dwell on the grace and mercy of God and to assure troubled people that God is kind. When I visited my stepmother in Manitoba several weeks before she died, she asked me earnestly if I thought God could possibly forgive her. What a joy it was to speak to her aching heart and say, "Yes, He will. He has forgiven me, and He will forgive you!"

I can remember persons saying, "It is all very well to say that God will save anybody, but you don't know me." Then I could say reassuringly, "Yes, but God does; and He has said, 'Whosoever will may come.'"

No one, however, can escape the undertone of warning that we find in the gospel message. When I open the door to heaven, I also open the door to hell. That sounds hard, but it is true.

When I was a new believer, I thought a great deal about such things. In fact, at one time I felt that I would be willing to forego heaven if it could possibly mean that others would not have to go to hell. But the way I felt did not make any difference. God has His own plans, and they must be considered.

Just how God will do this separating I do not know, but we are given a glimpse in the verses we are now considering. It would appear that God will allow the ungodly—those who reject the truth and enjoy doing evil—to become entrapped in falsehood. Such people will not even know what has happened to them. They will go through life thinking that they believe the right thing, but they will have strong delusions that cause them to believe a lie. It is dangerous to know the truth and to pass it by.

One can be gentle toward all people, reserved and sober in everything. But if one does not turn his heart toward God, he is in danger. It will do no good to think that this is unfair. This is the only world we know anything about, and God, who made this world and who made us, is the same yesterday, today, and forever. God wants you and me to trust in Him. If we do not do so, we are distinctly told what the result will be.

To take pleasure in ungodly things is dangerous. To delight in staying away from church services, not reading your Bible, and neglecting prayer can be catastrophic. We are told in the Book of Hebrews that "it is a fearful thing to fall into the hands of the living God."

But Paul goes on to talk about a pleasant, positive alternative to destruction:

> But we are bound to give thanks alway to God for you, brethren beloved of the Lord, because God hath from the beginning chosen you to salvation through sanctification of the Spirit and belief of the truth: whereunto he called you by our gospel, to the obtaining of the glory of our Lord Jesus Christ (2 Thess. 2:13–14).

If, when Paul says "we are bound to give thanks alway to God for you, brethren beloved of the Lord," you should feel that you are not good enough to be chosen, you have missed the point. Nobody is good enough: faith is what puts one in this category. By faith, I mean commitment to God. For faith is not only what one thinks, but also what one does with oneself. If you will turn yourself over to God, He will appoint you to salvation through sanctification of the Spirit and belief of the truth. Salvation will actually be in effect; something will really happen to you.

"Whereunto he called you by our gospel, to the obtaining of the glory of our Lord Jesus Christ." The fact that anyone ever believes is to God's credit. If He did not help me, I could not believe. How could a person come to faith on his own? God Himself cannot be seen; He is invisible. Nor do we come to faith through the processes of nature; God is not like that. He gives His Word for this purpose.

How then can one believe? Here is a wonderful thought: those who are *willing* to believe are given the grace to believe. Paul refers to these believers as his "brethren beloved of the Lord." They are called to obtain the glory of the Lord Jesus Christ: that is the fulfillment of His purpose. Believers in Christ are called to obtain forgiveness and peace and personal communion with God. They are called not only to eventual blessing in heaven, but to certain blessings in the here and now. God knew from the beginning who would heed His call in the course of events, but He calls by the gospel those who believe.

We have seen here that there is to be a final separation of the chaff from the wheat, of unbelievers from believers. Our hearts go out in grave concern for those who carelessly turn their backs on God, knowing that the end of their story is destruction. But we can also rejoice, knowing that whoever comes to the Lord Jesus Christ will in no wise be cast out.

BELIEVERS ARE HELPED TO STAND FAST
(2 Thess. 2:15–17)

Can you understand that it is because believers know God has planned to save them that they are inclined to hold fast to what they have been taught?

> Therefore, brethren, stand fast, and hold the traditions which ye have been taught, whether by word, or our epistle. Now our Lord Jesus Christ himself, and God, even our Father, which hath loved us, and hath given us everlasting consolation and good hope through grace, comfort your hearts, and stablish you in every good word and work (2 Thess. 2:15–17).

It is common for people to think that their future prospects depend on their own initiative. Ordinarily they feel that if anything is to happen tomorrow, they will have to do something about it. If their goal is not realized, they look for someone to blame. All this is only natural. But it is based on a wrong premise. As a matter of fact, much of what happens to them is due to circumstances over which they have little or no control. Moses expressed this well in the face of a great crisis in the Book of Exodus:

> And Moses said unto the people, Fear ye not, stand still, and see the salvation of the Lord, which he will show to you to day: for the Egyptians whom ye have seen to day, ye shall see them

again no more for ever. The Lord shall fight for you, and ye
shall hold your peace (Exod. 14:13–14).

In his letter to the Ephesians, Paul admonished these believers:

> Finally, my brethren, be strong in the Lord, and in the power
> of his might. Put on the whole armour of God, that ye may be
> able to stand against the wiles of the devil. For we wrestle not
> against flesh and blood, but against principalities, against powers,
> against the rulers of the darkness of this world, against
> spiritual wickedness in high places. Wherefore take unto you
> the whole armour of God, that ye may be able to withstand in
> the evil day, and having done all, to stand. Stand therefore,
> having your loins girt about with truth, and having on the
> breastplate of righteousness (Eph. 6:10–14).

In this second epistle to the Thessalonians, Paul has been
speaking about some very important matters. In view of what
he has just said about the coming end of the world, the return
of the Lord, the emergence of the man of sin, and the coming
in power of the antichrist who will attack Christians, believers
are urged to cling to the promises, the traditions. The first
promise they are to cling to is this:

> For God so loved the world, that he gave his only begotten
> Son, that whosoever believeth in him should not perish, but
> have everlasting life (John 3:16).

Believers should think of the Incarnation: of how God sent
His Son into this world to be born of woman, to be made
under the law, that He might do what was necessary to deliver
them. They should think of Calvary, where Christ went
to die for their sins. They should think of the Resurrection: of
the empty tomb, of how God raised Christ from the dead.
They should think of Pentecost: of how God sent His Holy
Spirit to dwell in the hearts of the believers. And they should
think of the return of the Lord. Those who cling to the gospel
should remember all these things.

Paul preached the gospel in his ministry. He preached
these promises, and the Thessalonians heard, and believed
them. They also rejoiced in them and witnessed to them in
the presence of other people.

Now Paul urges them to keep this up. He prays that the
Lord Himself, with the Father, will act to comfort and estab-

lish them. In writing about "our Lord Jesus Christ himself, and God, even our Father," he is not referring to the almighty creation power of God which is exercised on behalf of everybody, but to the personal relationship God has with those who believe in Him. He is their Father, the one who has loved them.

> But God commendeth his love toward us, in that, while we were yet sinners, Christ died for us (Rom. 5:8).

God our Father has not only loved us; He "hath given us everlasting consolation and good hope through grace." The "everlasting consolation" is comfort and assurance. "Good hope through grace" means hope for good things through God's grace, through His undeserved kindness and favor toward man.

Paul never forgot that we do not deserve these favors, but he rejoiced in the grace of God. He knew that God would do more for believers than they could ask or think. Now he called upon almighty God to do just that for the Thessalonians.

Finally Paul asked the Lord to "comfort your hearts, and stablish you in every good word and work."

Notice that the favor of God is within the believer: "comfort your hearts." The waves may mount high, the wind outside may blow, the thunder may roll and the lightning flash in the midst of the storm. But in the heart there is peace. There is quietness because God is with the believer and will take care of him.

"Stablish you (make you strong, settle you) in every good word and work." Whenever you see that word "establish," you may think of transplanting a plant. When you put a plant in a new place in the garden, you prepare the ground, water it, and then pack it around the roots. Then you expect that nature will take over and that the plant will grow as the roots reach out. When those roots reach out into the garden soil, the plant becomes established.

So it is that Paul prays for God to establish believers, to make them strong "in every good word and work." Believers do not do these works by chance; they do them because they belong to God and want to please Him. Their "roots" in Him make their testimony solid.

This passage is Paul's way of leading the Thessalonian believers to assurance in the face of all that he has been talking about. He has assured them that they can rest quietly and confidently and praise God. God is on their side; greater is He that is in them than he that is in the world.

SECOND THESSALONIANS
Chapter 3

† † †

BELIEVERS SHOULD PRAY FOR PREACHERS
(2 Thess. 3:1–5)

Do you understand that a believer is not expected to serve God in his own strength?

> Finally, brethren, pray for us, that the word of the Lord may have free course, and be glorified, even as it is with you: and that we may be delivered from unreasonable and wicked men: for all men have not faith (2 Thess. 3:1–2).

Serving the Lord in witnessing is very important, because it is through this activity that others are won to Him. Often, however, we are inclined to treat the individual believer as if he—not the Lord—were responsible for the outcome. We praise him when there are results, and we blame him when there are none. While this may be natural, it obscures the fact that "it is God which worketh in you both to will and to do of his good pleasure" (Phil. 2:13).

Paul had this truth in mind when he wrote these verses in 2 Thessalonians 3. He was not flexing his muscles and getting ready to show the world what he could do. He did not think that he would be smart enough to avoid evil or strong enough to get through difficulties on his own. He asked the Thessalonians to "pray for us."

Paul made two requests when he asked them to pray for him. The first was "that the Word of the Lord may have free course, and be glorified." Paul was anxious that the gospel not be hindered. Although he would do all that he could, he knew that there might be circumstances and conditions that he could not control. So he asked the Thessalonians to pray that God might overrule such things. Paul wanted the providence and grace of God to be in effect when he preached; he knew he needed that help.

The second was "that we may be delivered from unreasonable and wicked men." Paul wanted to escape the snares and traps that the opposition might set for him. He was aware that people might raise questions that could cause him to lose time, or present arguments that would be contrary to what he was teaching. He also knew that there were philosophies prevalent among educated people that could divert the message and destroy it. But Paul knew that a servant of God can proceed with confidence. He said:

> For I am not ashamed of the gospel of Christ: for it is the power
> of God unto salvation to every one that believeth (Rom. 1:16).

Nevertheless Paul was not overconfident; he knew that if there was any weak spot in his ministry, it was himself.

> But the Lord is faithful, who shall stablish you, and keep you
> from evil (2 Thess. 3:3).

It certainly helps the believer to be reconciled to God, to be able to look up to Him as Father, and to know that his soul is safe; but the believer also needs daily help in this world. Paul wanted the Thessalonians to know that the Lord, "who shall stablish you," would provide this daily help, confirming their faith, fixing their life style, and strengthening them.

"And keep you from evil." The believers were surrounded by all kinds of things that were contrary to the gospel, but God was on their side. It is wonderful to know that this is true for all believers, even when they are not thinking about it.

> And we have confidence in the Lord touching you, that ye both
> do and will do the things which we command you (2 Thess.
> 3:4).

Notice that Paul says, "we have confidence in the Lord touching you." He was not confident of their obedient response because they were so faithful or so good, but because the Lord was active in them and would carry them through.

> And the Lord direct your hearts into the love of God, and into
> the patient waiting for Christ (2 Thess. 3:5).

Here Paul's emphasis is not upon their minds or intellects, but upon their hearts. Deep down in their hearts, these people knew they were committed to God.

God is always working and challenging the believer's faith, prodding that person to look toward His return. The Lord is coming back, and believers should not think He is slack because He has waited this long.

BELIEVERS SHOULD BE CONCERNED ABOUT THE CONDUCT OF OTHER BELIEVERS
(2 Thess. 3:6–11)

Can you understand why the conduct of other believers is the proper concern of every believer?

> Now we command you, brethren, in the name of our Lord Jesus Christ, that ye withdraw yourselves from every brother that walketh disorderly, and not after the tradition which he received of us (2 Thess. 3:6).

The whole tone of the gospel of Jesus Christ is one of graciousness and generosity. God is unbelievably kind and gracious to us, and because we reflect something of His nature we are moved inwardly to be kind and gracious to others. He loves us, and so we love Him and others.

It is commonly felt that if we are true believers we should not judge anyone else. But this is an overstatement of a biblical principle. It is true that the Bible says, "Judge not, that ye be not judged" (Matt. 7:1). But in the same passage it is written, "Neither cast ye your pearls before swine (Matt. 7:6)." How will you obey that admonition unless you judge which people are the swine?

In Ephesians 4:32 Paul wrote: "And be ye kind one to another, tenderhearted, forgiving one another, even as God for Christ's sake hath forgiven you." We all recognize that this is in line with what the gospel requires. But in the above portion of Scripture we find a balancing note.

The above passage (2 Thess. 3:6) should make us somewhat sympathetic toward individual believers who feel that they need to withdraw from certain groups. There are people who may leave a prayer group or Bible class, or a congregation to which they have belonged all their lives, because they feel that the group now endorses things that are unscriptural. This, in part, is the ground on which they walk.

Some may think that such people are withdrawing from God's will. However, we cannot necessarily know what His will for them is. In any case, we need to remember that they are not withdrawing from Christ.

If you feel that you could never do this, or that God is not leading you to do it, you may praise the Lord. But suppose you feel the call to withdraw yourself from "every brother (believer) that walketh disorderly." Why withdraw from them? This might be done to avoid giving the appearance of approval.

The places I go are the places I endorse. At least, others may take it that way. If they see me going to a certain place for fellowship, they have a right to assume that I approve of the people there. John wrote about this in his second epistle:

> If there come any unto you, and bring not this doctrine, receive him not into your house, neither bid him God speed: for he that biddeth him God speed is partaker of his evil deeds (2 John 1:10–11).

But there is another side to the coin. I am reminded of a man who, upon several occasions, felt that he needed to withdraw from the congregation of which he had been a member for many years because the preacher was making statements that were not scriptural. Together we discussed the fact that God was in that church, that the Lord had given His name to it, and that He was bigger than the preacher. When this man was able to see that the congregation and what they represented were more important than the preacher, he went back to the church and accommodated himself to the situation.

Paul had heard strange stories about some in Thessalonica who did not work, but who expected to share his power. His response was to reiterate the principle that if a person does not work, he should not eat.

> For yourselves know how ye ought to follow us: for we behaved not ourselves disorderly among you; neither did we eat any

man's bread for nought; but wrought with labour and travail night and day, that we might not be chargeable to any of you: not because we have not power, but to make ourselves an example unto you to follow us. For even when we were with you, this we commanded you, that if any would not work, neither should he eat. For we hear that there are some which walk among you disorderly, working not at all, but are busybodies (2 Thess. 3:7–11).

The line of thought in this whole section needs to be handled with great care. Some people are naturally suspicious or critical of others, and we do not want to encourage that. But we also realize that the only way outsiders can know what we believe is by seeing where we stand and how we walk.

PEACE OF MIND IS A GREAT BLESSING
(2 Thess. 3:12–18)

Do you realize that one of the greatest blessings of God is peace of heart and mind?

Now them that are such (busybodies) we command and exhort by our Lord Jesus Christ, that with quietness they work, and eat their own bread. But ye, brethren, be not weary in well doing (2 Thess. 3:12–13).

Trouble is universal; everybody has it. We read in Job that man is born to trouble as the sparks fly upward. You may have troubles of your own. You may experience mutual troubles with others. Or you may be burdened by the troubles of your loved ones, which can weigh more heavily upon your heart than your own difficulties.

Trouble, like the waves of the sea, is always in motion. That is what makes the great invitation of the Lord Jesus Christ so appealing; "Come unto me, all ye that labour and are heavy laden, and I will give you rest" (Matt. 11:28). "Rest" is the word we need to hear when we are experiencing trouble. We need joy, too. But that comes after rest and peace.

Paul's epistle was an extension of his ministry designed to lead the believers into the fullness of blessing. He wanted those who had accepted Christ and were walking with Him to enter into rest, to have inward peace and quietness.

In the Thessalonian letters we have been studying, Paul has emphasized a number of important things: life after death, the return of the Lord, and—in its proper place—the judgment of God and the destruction of the wicked. The days of grace will one day come to an end as God acts to destroy the wicked. Before that time comes, Paul has pointed out, evil will become rampant. The enemy will even take on human form as the antichrist—the man of sin, master of deceit—and will be destroyed. Those will be dangerous days. Paul has written to inform the believers and to guide them. Always conveying the feeling that a word to the wise is sufficient, he is pointing out to willing people things that they could not know, but that he understands and wants to share with them.

Now, in the closing verses of 2 Thessalonians, we can feel Paul's quiet assurance. Many of the things he has been talking about have been disturbing, but notice how he addresses the busybodies. Paul exhorts them by our Lord Jesus Christ to quit disturbing others and work with quietness (a plain, clear, and positive word) to earn their own bread and make their own way.

> But ye, brethren, be not weary in well doing (2 Thess. 3:13).

When a person is doing right and others are not, it is tiring. When he works hard and gets no results, when he prays and prays and gets no apparent answers, it is exhausting. But Paul says, "Be not weary." He does not promise that things will work out or that the person will succeed; doing what is right may not result in any big consequences down here. The believer is to do the right thing because it is pleasing to God.

> And if any man obey not our word by this epistle, note that man, and have no company with him, that he may be ashamed (2 Thess. 3:14).

Let such a person know that you do not approve of what he is doing. You do not have to raise your voice and broadcast to the whole world how evil he is: you simply "have no company with him."

> Yet count him not as an enemy, but admonish him as a brother (2 Thess. 3:15).

To express disapproval but not scold or talk about the person to express disapproval but at the same time look upon him as your brother, takes real grace.

> Now the Lord of peace himself give you peace always by all means. The Lord be with you all (2 Thess. 3:16).

"The Lord of peace." What a wonderful thought! "Here "peace" means "inward quietness and confidence." At any time the Lord of peace can give the obedient believer this quietness and confidence.

> The salutation of Paul with mine own hand, which is the token in every epistle: so I write. The grace of our Lord Jesus Christ be with you all. Amen (2 Thess. 3:17–18).

We do not know all the details of Paul's physical condition. It may be that his eyesight was bad, because he dictated some of his epistles to other people. But apparently Paul made a practice of putting his own signature on each letter: "with mine own hand . . . so I write."

This is the way Paul ends his epistle: "The grace of our Lord Jesus Christ be with you all. Amen." Paul simply indicates that believers are to be blessed with the grace of the Lord. That is the will of God, and we praise His holy name for it.

May you be helped in your own heart and mind to yield yourself to him, following His guidance, trusting in and counting on Him. He wants you to have peace.